D0102913

SIDE *by* SIDE

SECOND EDITION

BOOK 1

Steven J. Molinsky / Bill Bliss

PRENTICE HALL REGENTS
Englewood Cliffs, NJ 07632

Library of Congress Cataloging-in-Publication Data

Molinsky, Steven J.
    Side by side / Steven J. Molinsky, Bill Bliss. — 2nd ed.
        pp. 160

    ISBN 0-13-811076-X (v. 1)
    1. English language—Conversation and phrase books.   2. English
language—Textbooks for foreign speakers.   I. Bliss, Bill.
II. Title.
PE1131.M58 1989   88-22455
428.3′4—dc19   CIP

Editorial/production supervision: Janet Johnston
Art supervision: Diane Koromhas
Manufacturing buyers: Art Michalez, Laura Crossland
Cover design: Kenny Beck

Illustrated by Richard E. Hill

 © 1989 by Prentice Hall Regents
Prentice-Hall, Inc.
A Division of Simon & Schuster
Englewood Cliffs, New Jersey 07632

Printed in the United States of America

20 19

ISBN 0-13-811076-X

Prentice-Hall International (UK) Limited, *London*
Prentice-Hall of Australia Pty. Limited, *Sydney*
Prentice-Hall Canada Inc., *Toronto*
Prentice-Hall Hispanoamericana, S.A., *Mexico*
Prentice-Hall of India Private Limited, *New Delhi*
Prentice-Hall of Japan, Inc., *Tokyo*
Simon & Schuster Asia Pte. Ltd., *Singapore*
Editora Prentice-Hall do Brasil, Ltda., *Rio de Janeiro*

CONTENTS

To Be: Introduction ▪

What's Your Name?

*What's = What is
†235 = two thirty-five
**741–8906 = seven four one – eight nine "oh" six

Answer these questions.

1. What's your name?

   My name is Julia Salamanca

2. What's your address?

   My address is 5666 Deodar St
   Montclair, CA 91763

3. What's your phone number?

   My phone number is 460-9879

4. Where are you from?

   I from México city

Now ask other students in your class.

ON YOUR OWN: Interview

Interview a famous person. Make up addresses, phone numbers, and cities. Use your imagination. Role play these interviews in class.

A. What's your name?

B. My name is _Robert Aguilar_.

A. _What's your_ address?

B. _My adres is 2625 Main street._

A. _What's your_ phone number?

B. _My phone (909) 985 5675_.

A. Where are you from?

B. _I'm from Guadalajara, Jal._

a famous actor

a famous actress

a famous athlete

the president/prime minister of your country

WHAT'S YOUR NAME?

My name is David Miller. I'm American. I'm from New York.

My name is Mrs. White. My phone number is 237–5976.

My name is Susan Black. My address is 378 Main Street, Waterville, Florida. My license number is 112897.

My name is Mr. Taylor. My apartment number is 3–B.

My name is William Chen. My address is 694 River Street, Brooklyn, New York. My telephone number is 469–7750. My Social Security number is 044-35-9862.

CHECK-UP

Match

<u>c</u> 1. name

<u>e</u> 2. address

<u>a</u> 3. phone number

<u>b</u> 4. apartment number

<u>d</u> 5. Social Security number

a. 237–5976

b. 3–B

c. William Chen

d. 044-35-9862

e. 378 Main Street

Listening

Listen and choose the best answer.

1. a. Mrs. White
   b. Susan Miller

2. a. 394 Main Street
   b. 394 River Street

3. a. 9–D
   b. 9–B

4. a. 748–2066
   b. 748–2260

5. a. 060-83-8752
   b. 060-83-8275

IN YOUR OWN WORDS

Fill out the form.

ACME COMPANY
Employment Application Form

Name *Susan Miller*

Address *394 River Street*
9 B

Telephone Number *748 - 2260*

Social Security Number *060-83-8275*

CHAPTER 1   *SUMMARY*

GRAMMAR

To Be

am	I'm from Mexico City. (I am)
is	What's your name? (What is)
	My name is Maria.
are	Where are you from?

FUNCTIONS

Asking for and Reporting Information

What's your name?
  My name is *Maria*.
What's your address?
  My address is *235 Main Street*.
What's your phone number?
  My phone number is *741–8906*.
Where are you from?
  I'm from *Mexico City*.

I'm *American*.

My license number is *112897*.
My apartment number is *3-B*.
My Social Security number is *044-35-9862*.

To Be + Location ■
Subject Pronouns ■

At Home

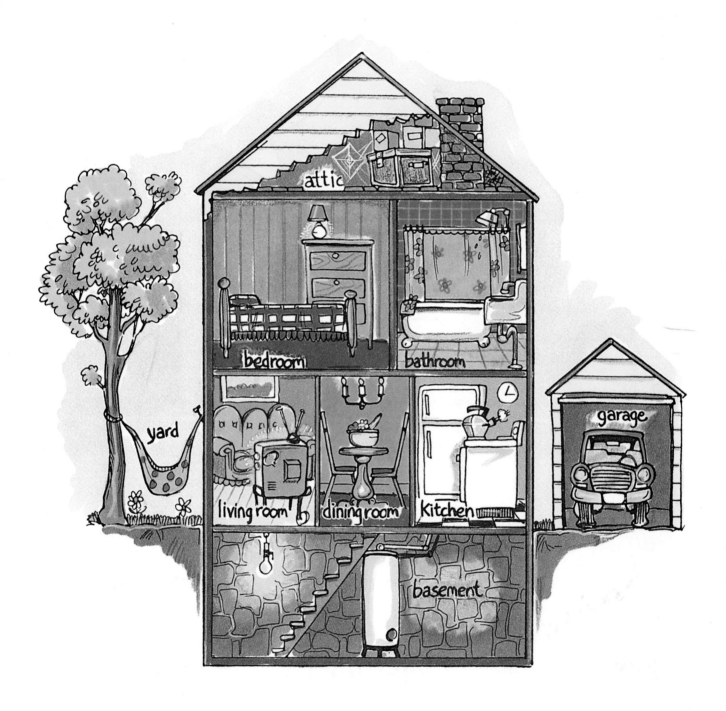

attic

bedroom

bathroom

yard

living room

dining room

kitchen

garage

basement

Where Are You?

(I am)	I'm	
(He is)	He's	
(She is)	She's	in the kitchen.
(It is)	It's	
(We are)	We're	
(You are)	You're	
(They are)	They're	

Where	am	I	?
	is	he / she / it	
	are	we / you / they	

1. Where are you?

2. Where are you?

3. Where are you?

4. Where are you?

5. Where are Bill and Mary?

6. Where are Mr. and Mrs. Wilson?

7. Where are you?

8. Where are you and Tom?

9. Where are Mr. and Mrs. Johnson?

Where's Bob?

*Where's = Where is

1. Where's Tom?

2. Where's Fred?

3. Where's Helen?

4. Where's Betty?

5. Where's the newspaper?

6. Where's the cat?

7. Where's Jane?

8. Where's John?

9. Where's the dog?

THE STUDENTS IN MY ENGLISH CLASS

The students in my English class are very interesting. Henry is Chinese. He's from Shanghai. Natasha is Russian. She's from Leningrad. Mr. and Mrs. Ramirez are Puerto Rican. They're from San Juan.

George is Greek. He's from Athens. Nicole is French. She's from Paris. Mr. and Mrs. Sato are Japanese. They're from Tokyo. My friend Maria and I are Mexican. We're from Mexico City.

Yes, the students in my English class are very interesting. We're from many different countries . . . and we're friends.

 *CHECK-UP*

True or False?

1. Nicole is Greek.
2. Natasha is Russian.
3. Henry is from Mexico City.
4. Mr. Sato is from Tokyo.
5. Mrs. Ramirez is Chinese.
6. The students in the class are from many countries.

How about YOU?

Tell about the students in YOUR English class. Where are they from?

Where Are They?

Ask and answer questions based on these pictures.

1. _Where's_ Albert?
He's in the Restaurant.

2. _Where's_ Carmen?
She's in the Bank.

3. _Where's_ Walter and Mary?
They're in the _____.
supermarket.

4. _Were are_ you?
I am in The library

5. _Were are_ you?
We're in the Park

6. _Where's_ Rita?
She is in The Movie theater.

7. _Where are_ Mr. and Mrs. Jones?
There are in the Post office.

8. _Where is_ the monkey?
It is in The Zoo.

9. _____ I?
_____.

Now add people and places of your own.

10. _____?
_____.

11. _____?
_____.

12. _____?
_____.

ALL THE STUDENTS IN MY ENGLISH CLASS ARE ABSENT TODAY

All the students in my English class are absent today. George is absent. He's in the hospital. Maria is absent. She's at the dentist. Mr. and Mrs. Sato are absent. They're at the Social Security office. Even our English teacher is absent. He's home in bed!

What a shame! Everybody in my English class is absent today. Everybody except me.

✔ CHECK-UP

Answer These Questions

1. Where's George?
2. Where's Maria?
3. Where are Mr. and Mrs. Sato?
4. Where's the English teacher?

Listening

Listen and choose the best answer.

1. a. bank   b. park
2. a. hospital   b. library
3. a. He's   b. She's
4. a. He's   b. She's
5. a. We're   b. They're
6. a. We're   b. They're

How about YOU?

Tell about YOUR English class:
   Which students are in class today?
   Which students are absent today?
   Where are they?

CHAPTER 2 *SUMMARY*

GRAMMAR

Subject Pronouns
To Be + Location

Where	am	I?
	is	he? she? it?
	are	we? you? they?

(I am)	I'm	
(He is) (She is) (It is)	He's She's It's	in the kitchen.
(We are) (You are) (They are)	We're You're They're	

FUNCTIONS

Asking for and Reporting Information

Henry is *Chinese.*
He's from *Shanghai.*

Inquiring about Location

Where are you?

Giving Location

I'm in the *kitchen.*

Present Continuous Tense ◾

What Are You Doing?

(I am)	I'm	
(He is)	He's	
(She is)	She's	} eating.
(It is)	It's	
(We are)	We're	
(You are)	You're	
(They are)	They're	

	am	I	
What	is	{ he she it }	doing?
	are	{ we you they }	

Complete these conversations.

1. **A.** What are you doing?
   B. _____ reading the newspaper.

2. **A.** _____ Mr. and Mrs. Jones doing?
   B. _____ eating dinner.

3. **A.** _____ Henry doing?
   B. _____ cooking dinner.

4. **A.** _____ Maria doing?
   B. _____ studying English.

5. **A.** _____ Frank doing?
   B. _____ sleeping.

6. **A.** _____ Sam and Betty doing?
   B. _____ watching TV.

7. **A.** _____ Judy doing?
   B. _____ playing the piano.

8. **A.** What are YOU doing?
   B. I'm _____.

What's Everybody Doing?

A. Where's Walter?

B. He's in the kitchen.

A. What's he doing?

B. He's eating breakfast.

1. *Betty*
   park
   eating lunch

2. *Mr. and Mrs. Smith*
   dining room
   eating dinner

3. *you*
   bedroom
   playing the guitar

4. *you*
   living room
   playing cards

5. Tom and Mary
   yard
   playing baseball

6. Miss Jackson
   restaurant
   drinking coffee

7. Mr. Larson
   cafeteria
   drinking lemonade

8. you
   library
   studying English

9. Tommy
   classroom
   studying mathematics

10. Gloria
    night club
    dancing

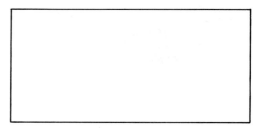

11. Harry
    bathroom
    singing

12. Barbara
    hospital
    watching TV

13. you
    park
    listening to the radio

14.

IN THE PARK

The Jones family is in the park today. The sun is shining and the birds are singing. It's a beautiful day!

Mr. Jones is reading the newspaper. Mrs. Jones is listening to the radio. Sally and Patty Jones are studying. And Tommy Jones is playing the guitar.

The Jones family is very happy today. It's a beautiful day and they're in the park.

AT HOME IN THE YARD

The Smith family is at home in the yard today. The sun is shining and the birds are singing. It's a beautiful day!

Mr. Smith is planting flowers. Mrs. Smith is drinking lemonade and reading a book. Mary and Billy Smith are playing with the dog. And Sam Smith is sleeping.

The Smith family is very happy today. It's a beautiful day and they're at home in the yard.

CHECK-UP

True or False?

1. The Jones family is at home in the yard today.
2. Mr. Smith is planting flowers.
3. Sally Jones is studying.
4. Billy Smith is reading a book.
5. The Smith family is singing.
6. The Jones family and the Smith family are very happy today.

Listening

Listen and choose the best answer.

1. a. She's reading.
   b. I'm reading.

2. a. He's cooking.
   b. She's cooking.

3. a. He's watching TV.
   b. She's watching TV.

4. a. We're studying.
   b. They're studying.

5. a. We're eating.
   b. They're eating.

6. a. You're drinking lemonade.
   b. We're drinking lemonade.

Q & A

Using this model, make questions and answers based on the stories on page 20.

A. What's *Mr. Jones* doing?
B. *He's reading the newspaper.*

IN YOUR OWN WORDS

For Writing and Discussion

AT THE BEACH

The Martinez family is at the beach today. Using this picture, tell a story about the Martinez family.

CHAPTER 3 *SUMMARY*

GRAMMAR

Present Continuous Tense

What	am	I	doing?
	is	he she it	
	are	we you they	

(I am)	I'm	eating.
(He is) (She is) (It is)	He's She's It's	
(We are) (You are) (They are)	We're You're They're	

FUNCTIONS

Asking for and Reporting Information

What are you doing?
　I'm *reading*.

What's *Mr. Jones* doing?
　He's *reading the newspaper*.

Inquiring about Location

Where's *Walter?*

Giving Location

He's in the *kitchen*.

To Be: Short Answers
Possessive Adjectives

I'm Fixing My Sink

I	my
he	his
she	her
it	its
we	our
you	your
they	their

Are You Busy?

I	am.
Yes, { he / she / it }	is.
{ we / you / they }	are.

1. Is Nancy busy?
washing her car

2. Is Ted busy?
feeding his dog

3. Are you busy?
cleaning our yard

4. Are Mr. and Mrs. Jones busy?
painting their kitchen

5. Are you busy?
doing my homework

6. Is Alan busy?
doing his exercises

7. **Is Linda busy?**
fixing her bicycle

8. **Are you busy?**
cleaning our apartment

9. **Are Bob and Judy busy?**
washing their windows

10. **Is Pedro busy?**
feeding his cat

11. **Are you busy?**
washing my clothes

12. **Are you busy?**
fixing our TV

13. **Is Henry busy?**
cleaning his garage

14. **Are your children busy?**
brushing their teeth

Use this model to talk about the picture with other students in your class.

A. Where's Miss Johnson?

B. She's in the parking lot.

A. What's she doing?

B. She's washing her car.

A BUSY DAY

Everybody at 149 River Street is very busy today. Mr. Anderson is cleaning his kitchen. Mrs. Wilson is fixing her kitchen sink. Mr. and Mrs. Thomas are painting their living room. Mrs. Black is doing her exercises. Tommy Lee is feeding his dog. And Mr. and Mrs. Lane are washing their car.

I'm busy, too. I'm washing my windows . . . and of course, I'm watching all my neighbors. It's a very busy day at 149 River Street.

CHECK-UP

True or False?

1. Mr. Anderson is in his kitchen.
2. Tommy is eating.
3. Mr. and Mrs. Lane are in their apartment.
4. Mrs. Thomas is painting.
5. Their address is 147 River Street.

Q & A

Using this model, make questions and answers based on the story.

A. What's *Mr. Anderson* doing?
B. *He's cleaning his kitchen.*

Listening

Listen and choose the best answer.

1. a. My kitchen.
   b. My homework.

2. a. The piano.
   b. Lemonade.

3. a. The newspaper.
   b. Dinner.

4. a. A book.
   b. Breakfast.

5. a. TV.
   b. His clothes.

6. a. My windows.
   b. The birds.

IN YOUR OWN WORDS

For Writing and Discussion

A BUSY DAY

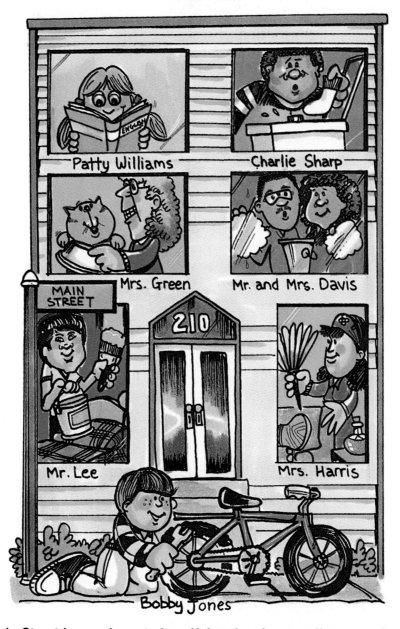

Everybody at 210 Main Street is very busy today. Using the picture, tell a story about them.

CHAPTER 4 *SUMMARY*

GRAMMAR

To Be: Short Answers

Yes,	I	am.
	he she it	is.
	we you they	are.

Possessive Adjectives

I'm He's She's It's We're You're They're	cleaning	**my** **his** **her** **its** **our** **your** **their**	room.

FUNCTIONS

Greeting People

Hi!

Asking for and Reporting Information

What are you doing?
  I'm *fixing my sink*.

Are you busy?
  Yes, I am. I'm *washing my hair*.

Inquiring about Location

Where's *Miss Johnson?*

Giving Location

She's in the *parking lot*.

To Be:
  Yes/No Questions ■
  Short Answers ■
Adjectives ■
Possessive Nouns ■

Tall or Short?

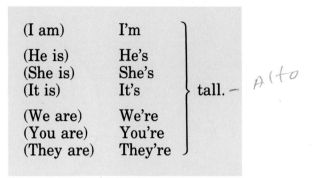

(I am)	I'm
(He is)	He's
(She is)	She's
(It is)	It's
(We are)	We're
(You are)	You're
(They are)	They're

} tall. — *Alto*

A. Is Bob tall or short?

B. He's tall.

A. Is Bill tall or short?

B. He's short.

largo — *tall*   *short* — *chaparro*

Ask and answer these questions.

Alice — *young — joven*

Margaret — *vieja — old*

Herman — *heavy fat — gordo*

David — *flaco — thin*

1. Is Alice young or old?

2. Is Margaret young or old?

3. Is Herman heavy or thin?

4. Is David fat or thin?

Herman's car — *new — nuevo*

David's car — *viejo — old*

Betty — *beautiful — maravillosa pretty — bonita*

Hilda — *fea — ugly*

5. Is Herman's car new or old?

6. Is David's car new or old?

7. Is Betty beautiful or ugly?

8. Is Hilda pretty or ugly?

Edward — handsome - *guapo*   Captain Blood — *feo* - ugly

Albert — rich *rico*   John — *pobre* poor

9. Is Edward handsome or ugly?

10. Is Captain Blood handsome or ugly?

11. Is Albert rich or poor?

12. Is John rich or poor?

Albert's house — large - *grande* / big *grande*   John's apartment — *pequeño* small / *pequeño* little

Mary's neighbors — noisy / loud - *ruidoso*   Jane's neighbors — *quieto* quiet

13. Is Albert's house large or small?

14. Is John's apartment big or little?

15. Are Mary's neighbors noisy or quiet?

16. Are Jane's neighbors loud or quiet?

expensive - *caro* / *barato*   cheap

Barbara — married   Julie — single

casada   soltera

17. Is champagne expensive or cheap?

18. Is tea expensive or cheap?

19. Is Barbara married or single?

20. Is Julie married or single?

easy - *fácil*   *dificultad* difficult

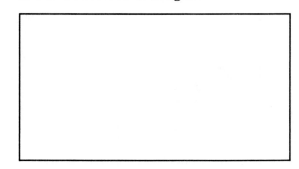

21. Are the questions in Chapter 5 easy or difficult?

22. Are the questions in Chapter 17 easy or difficult?

Now ask and answer questions of your own.

Tell Me About . . .

Am	I		
Is	{ he she it		tall?
Are	{ we you they		

	I	am.
Yes,	he she it }	is.
	we you they }	are.

	I'm	not.
No,	he she it }	isn't.
	we you they }	aren't.

Are you married?

No, I'm not. I'm single.

Tell me about your new car. Is it large?

No, it isn't. It's small.

Tell me about your new neighbors. Are they quiet?

No, they aren't. They're noisy.

1. A. Tell me about your brother.

_____ _____ tall?

B. No, _____. _____.

2. A. Tell me about your sister.

_____ _____ single?

B. No, _____. _____.

34

3. A. Tell me about your apartment.

_____ _____ new?

B. No, _____ . _____ .

4. A. Tell me about your new boss.

_____ _____ old?

B. No, He is . _____ .

5. A. Tell me about Stanley's Restaurant.

_____ _____ expensive?

B. No, is . _____ .

6. A. Tell me about your neighbors.

_____ _____ noisy?

B. No, _____ . _____ .

7. A. Tell me about Henry's cat.

_____ _____ pretty?

B. No, _____ . _____ .

8. A. Tell me about Fred and Sally's dog.

_____ _____ little?

B. No, is . _____ .

9. A. Tell me about the questions in your English book.

_____ _____ difficult?

B. No, _____ . _____ .

10. A. Tell me about Santa Claus.

_____ _____ thin?

B. No, _____ . _____ .

The Weather

It's sunny.

It's cloudy.

It's raining.

It's snowing.

It's hot.

It's warm.

It's cool.

It's cold.

How's the weather today in YOUR city?

ON YOUR OWN: A Long Distance Telephone Call

A. Hi, Jack. This is Jim. I'm calling from Miami.

B. From Miami? What are you doing in Miami?

A. I'm on vacation.

B. How's the weather in Miami? Is it sunny?

A. No, it isn't. It's raining.

B. Is it hot?

A. No, it isn't. It's cold.

B. Are you having a good time?

A. No, I'm not. I'm having a TERRIBLE time. The weather is TERRIBLE here.

B. I'm sorry to hear that.

A. Hi, _____. This is _____. I'm calling from _____.

B. From _____? What are you doing in _____?

A. I'm on vacation.

B. How's the weather in _____? Is it _____?

A. No, it isn't. It's _____.

B. Is it _____?

A. No, it isn't. It's _____.

B. Are you having a good time?

A. No, I'm not. I'm having a TERRIBLE time. The weather is TERRIBLE here.

B. I'm sorry to hear that.

1. *Switzerland*
   cool?
   snowing?

2. *Honolulu*
   hot?
   sunny?

You're on vacation and the weather is terrible. Call a student in your class. Use the conversation above as a guide.

DEAR MOTHER

Royal Sludge Hotel

Dear Mother,

I'm writing to you from our hotel at Sludge Beach. Ralph and I are on vacation with the children for a few days. We're happy to be here, but to tell the truth, we're having a few problems.

The weather isn't very good. In fact, it's cold and cloudy. Right now I'm looking out the window and it's raining cats and dogs.

The children aren't very happy. In fact, they're bored and they're having a terrible time. Right now they're sitting on the bed, playing cards and watching TV.

The restaurants here are expensive, and the food isn't very good. In fact, Ralph is at the doctor's office right now. He's having problems with his stomach.

All the other hotels here are beautiful and new. Our hotel is ugly, and it's very, very old. In fact, right now a repairman is fixing the toilet.

As you can see, Mother, we're having a few problems here at Sludge Beach, but we're happy. We're happy to be on vacation, and we're happy to be together.

See you soon.

Love,
Ethel

 CHECK-UP

True or False?

1. The weather is beautiful.
2. The children are swimming.
3. Their hotel is old.
4. A repairman is fixing the window.
5. Ralph isn't at the hotel right now.
6. Ethel is watching the cats and dogs.

Listening

Listen and choose the best answer.

1. a. It's old.   b. It's sunny.
2. a. It's small.   b. It's bored.
3. a. They're noisy.   b. They're new.
4. a. He's cloudy.   b. He's handsome.
5. a. It's large.   b. It's fat.
6. a. It's easy.   b. It's beautiful.

CHAPTER 5 *SUMMARY*

GRAMMAR

To Be: Yes/No Questions

Am	I	
Is	he she it	tall?
Are	we you they	

To Be: Short Answers

	I	am.
Yes,	he she it	is.
	we you they	are.

	I'm	not.
No,	he she it	isn't.
	we you they	aren't.

Adjectives

tall	short
young	old
new	old
heavy/fat	thin
beautiful/pretty/ handsome	ugly
rich	poor
large	small
big	little
loud/noisy	quiet
expensive	cheap
married	single
easy	difficult

Possessive Nouns

Is Albert**'s** house large or small?
Are Mary**'s** neighbors noisy or quiet?

FUNCTIONS

Asking for and Reporting Information

Is *Bob tall* or *short?*
  He's tall.

Tell me about *your new car.*

I'm calling from *Miami.*

What are you doing *in Miami?*

How's the weather *in Miami?*
  It's *raining.*

Is it *hot?*
  No, it isn't. It's *cold.*

Describing

He's *tall.*

Greeting People

Hi, *Jack.* This is *Jim.*

Expressing Dissatisfaction

I'm having a terrible time.

Sympathizing

I'm sorry to hear that.

To Be: Review ■
Present Continuous Tense: Review ■
Prepositions of Location ■

My Favorite Photographs

A. Who is he?

B. He's my father.

A. What's his name?

B. His name is Paul.

A. Where is he?

B. He's in Paris.

A. What's he doing?

B. He's standing in front of the Eiffel Tower.

Using these questions, talk about the following photographs.

Who is he/she? (Who are they?)

What _____ name (names)?

Where _____?

What _____ doing?

1. *my wife*
   in New York
   standing in front of the
   Statue of Liberty

2. *my son*
   in the park
   playing soccer

3. *my daughter*
   in her bedroom
   sleeping

4. *my husband*
   at the beach
   swimming (suiming)

5. *my sister and brother*
   at our house
   standing in front of the fireplace

6. *my mother*
   in our living room
   sitting on the sofa and
   watching TV

7. *my aunt and uncle*
   in their dining room
   having dinner

8. *my cousin*
   in front of his apartment building
   washing his car

9. *my grandmother and grandfather*
   at my wedding
   crying

10. *my cousin*
    in the park
    sitting on a bench and
    feeding the birds

11. *my friend*
sitting on his bed
playing the guitar

12. *my wife's brother**
in Washington
standing in front of the
Washington Monument

13. *my brother's wife†*
in their apartment
painting their living room

14. *my friends*
at my birthday party
singing and dancing

*wife's brother = brother-in-law
†brother's wife = sister-in-law

ON YOUR OWN: Your Favorite Photographs

This is a picture of my brother and me. My brother's name is Carlos. We're sitting in the living room of our apartment. Carlos is playing the piano and I'm playing the guitar.

Bring in your favorite photographs to class. Talk about them with other students. Ask the other students about *their* favorite photographs.

ARTHUR IS VERY ANGRY

It's late at night. Arthur is sitting on his bed and he's looking at his clock. His neighbors are making a lot of noise, and Arthur is VERY angry.

The people in Apartment 2 are dancing. The man in Apartment 3 is vacuuming the carpet in his living room. The woman in Apartment 4 is practicing the violin. The teenagers in Apartment 5 are listening to loud rock music. The dog in Apartment 6 is barking. And the people in Apartment 7 are having a big argument.

It's very late and Arthur is tired and angry. What a terrible night!

CHECK-UP

Q & A

Using this model, make questions and answers based on the story.

A. What's *the man in Apartment 3* doing?
B. *He's vacuuming the carpet in his living room.*

Choose

1. Arthur's neighbors are
   a. noisy.
   b. angry.

2. The man in Apartment 3 is
   a. painting his apartment.
   b. cleaning his apartment.

3. The noisy people in Apartment 5 are
   a. young.
   b. old.

4. The dog in Apartment 6 isn't
   a. sleeping.
   b. making noise.

5. The woman in Apartment 4 is
   a. playing cards.
   b. playing music.

6. Arthur isn't very
   a. happy.
   b. tired.

TOM'S WEDDING DAY

Today is a very special day. It's my wedding day, and all my family and friends are here. Everybody is having a wonderful time.

My wife, Jane, is standing in front of the fireplace. She's wearing a beautiful white wedding gown. Uncle Harry is taking her photograph, and Aunt Emma is crying. (She's very sentimental.)

The band is playing my favorite popular music. My mother is dancing with Jane's father, and Jane's mother is dancing with my father.

My sister and Jane's brother are standing in the yard, eating wedding cake and talking about politics. Our grandparents are sitting in the corner, drinking champagne and talking about "the good old days."

Everybody is having a good time. People are singing, dancing, and laughing, and our families are getting to know each other. It's a very special day.

✓ CHECK-UP

Answer These Questions

1. Where is Jane standing?
2. What's she wearing?
3. What's Uncle Harry doing?
4. What's Aunt Emma doing?
5. What are Tom's sister and Jane's brother doing?
6. What are their grandparents doing?

Listening: *Quiet or Noisy?*

Listen to the sentence. Are the people quiet or noisy?

1. a. quiet   b. noisy
2. a. quiet   b. noisy
3. a. quiet   b. noisy
4. a. quiet   b. noisy
5. a. quiet   b. noisy
6. a. quiet   b. noisy

IN YOUR OWN WORDS

For Writing and Discussion

JENNIFER'S BIRTHDAY PARTY

Today is a very special day. It's Jennifer's birthday party, and all her family and friends are there. Using this picture, tell a story about her party.

CHAPTER 6 *SUMMARY*

GRAMMAR

To Be

Who is	he? she?
Who are	they?

He's my father. She's my wife.
They're my aunt and uncle.

Present Continuous Tense

What's	he she	doing?
What are	they	doing?

He's She's	playing soccer.
They're	having dinner.

Prepositions of Location

in	He's in Paris. She's in her bedroom.
at	He's at the beach. They're at my wedding.
on	She's sitting on the sofa.
in front of	He's in front of his house.

FUNCTIONS

Asking for and Reporting Information

Who is he?
  He's *my father*.
What's his name?
  His name is *Paul*.
What's he doing?
  He's *standing in front of the Eiffel Tower*.

Inquiring about Location

Where is *he?*

Giving Location

He's in Paris.

Prepositions ▪
There Is/There Are ▪
Singular/Plural:
Introduction ▪

Where's the Restaurant?

A. Where's the restaurant?
B. It's **next to** the bank.

A. Where's the school?
B. It's **between** the library and the park.

A. Where's the supermarket?
B. It's **across from** the movie theater.

A. Where's the post office?
B. It's **around the corner from** the hospital.

1. Where's the park?

2. Where's the bank?

3. Where's the church?

4. Where's the movie theater?

5. Where's the restaurant?

6. Where's the police station?

7. Where's the fire station?

8. Where's the post office?

Is There a Laundromat in This Neighborhood?

> **There's (There is)** a bank on Main Street.
> **Is there** a bank on Main Street?

A. Excuse me. Is there a laundromat in this neighborhood?*

B. Yes. There's a laundromat on Main Street, next to the supermarket.

*Or: Is there a laundromat nearby?

1. *post office?*

2. *bank?*

3. *movie theater?*

4. *gas station?*

5. *bus station?*

6. *cafeteria?*

7. *drug store?*

8. *library?*

ON YOUR OWN: What's in Your Neighborhood?

Is there . . . ?   Yes, there is.
No, there isn't.

Draw a simple map of your neighborhood. With another student, ask and answer questions about your neighborhoods. Here are some places you can include in your questions:

bakery	church	gas station	police station
bank	clinic	hospital	post office
barber shop	department store	laundromat	restaurant
beauty parlor	doctor's office	library	school
bus station	drug store	movie theater	supermarket
cafeteria	fire station	park	train station

Is There a Stove in the Kitchen?

A. Is there a stove in the kitchen?

B. Yes, there is. There's a very nice stove in the kitchen.

A. Oh, good.

A. Is there a refrigerator in the kitchen?

B. No, there isn't.

A. Oh, I see.

1. *a closet in the bedroom?*
   Yes, . . .

2. *an elevator in the building?*
   No, . . .

3. *a window in the kitchen?*
   Yes, . . .

4. *a fire escape?*
   No, . . .

5. *a superintendent in the building?*
   No, . . .

6. *a jacuzzi in the bathroom?*
   Yes, . . .

How Many Bedrooms Are There in the Apartment?

How many windows **are there** in the bedroom?

There's one window in the bedroom.
There are two windows in the bedroom.

A. Tell me, how many bedrooms are there in the apartment?

B. There are two bedrooms in the apartment.

A. Two bedrooms?

B. Yes. That's right.

1. *windows*
   living room

2. *floors*
   building

3. *closets*
   apartment

4. *apartments*
   building

5. *bathrooms*
   apartment

6. *washing machines*
   basement

ON YOUR OWN: Looking for an Apartment

a student a room an exercise	Yes, there is. No, there isn't.	students rooms exercises	Yes, there are. No, there aren't.

You're looking for a new apartment. Another student in your class is the landlord. Ask the landlord about the apartment on page 55.

1. Is there a stove in the kitchen?
2. Is there a refrigerator in the kitchen?
3. Is there a superintendent in the building?
4. Is there an elevator in the building?
5. Is there a fire escape?
6. Is there a TV antenna on the roof?
7. Is there a radiator in every room?
8. Is there a mailbox near the building?
9. Is there a bus stop near the building?
10. Are there any pets in the building?

11. Are there any children in the building?
12. How many rooms are there in the apartment?
13. How many floors are there in the building?
14. How many closets are there in the bedroom?
15. How many windows are there in the living room?

Ask the landlord some other questions.

_____
_____
_____

Are there any problems in the apartment on page 55? Don't ask the landlord! Another student in your class is a tenant in the building. Ask that student.

16. Are there any mice in the basement?
17. Are there any cockroaches in the apartment?

18. Are there any broken windows?
19. Are there any holes in the walls?

Ask the tenant some other questions.

_____
_____
_____

THE NEW SHOPPING MALL

Everybody in Brewster is talking about the city's new shopping mall. The mall is outside the city, next to the Brewster airport. There are more than one hundred stores in the mall.

There are two big department stores. There are many clothing stores for men, women, and children. There's a very big toy store. There are two shoe stores, two drug stores, and four restaurants. There's even a movie theater.

Almost all the people in Brewster are happy that their city's new shopping mall is now open. But some people aren't happy. The owners of the small stores in the old center of town are very upset. They're upset because there aren't many people shopping in their stores in the center of town. They're all shopping at the new mall.

CHECK-UP

Choose

1. Everybody in Brewster is
   a. at the airport.
   b. outside the city.
   c. talking about the mall.

2. In the mall, there are
   a. two toy stores.
   b. two drug stores.
   c. two restaurants.

3. In the mall,
   a. there are toy stores and shoe stores.
   b. there are restaurants and drug stores.
   c. there are clothing stores and movie theaters.

4. The store owners in the center of town are upset because
   a. people aren't shopping in their stores.
   b. people aren't shopping at the mall.
   c. they're very old.

How about YOU?

Is there a shopping mall in your city or town?
Are there small stores in your city or town?
Tell about the stores where you live.

JANE'S APARTMENT BUILDING

Jane's apartment building is in the center of town. Jane is very happy there because the building is in a very convenient place.

Across from the building, there's a laundromat, a bank, and a post office. Next to the building, there's a drug store and a restaurant. Around the corner from the building, there are two gas stations.

There's a lot of noise near Jane's apartment building. There are a lot of cars on the street, and there are a lot of people walking on the sidewalk all day and all night.

Jane isn't very upset about the noise, though. Her building is in the center of town. It's a very busy place, but for Jane, it's a very convenient place to live.

CHECK-UP

Answer These Questions

1. Where is Jane's apartment building?
2. What's across from her building?
3. Is there a drug store near her building?
4. Why is there a lot of noise near Jane's building?
5. Why is Jane happy there?

True or False?

1. Jane's apartment is in a very convenient place.
2. There's a laundromat around the corner from her building.
3. Two gas stations are nearby.
4. There are a lot of cars on the sidewalk.
5. The center of town is very noisy.

Listening

What words do you hear?

Example (a.) park   b.   shoe store   (c.) drug store

1.   a.   park   b.   bank   c.   restaurant
2.   a.   police station   b.   gas station   c.   fire station
3.   a.   supermarket   b.   department store   c.   school
4.   a.   toy store   b.   two toy stores   c.   movie theater
5.   a.   bank   b.   clothing store   c.   shoe store

 *IN YOUR OWN WORDS*_____

For Writing and Discussion

GEORGE'S APARTMENT BUILDING

George's apartment building is in the center of town. George is very happy there because the building is in a very convenient place. Using the picture, tell about George's neighborhood.

How about YOU?

Tell about YOUR neighborhood:
Is it convenient? Is it very busy?
Is it noisy or quiet?

CHAPTER 7 *SUMMARY*

GRAMMAR

Prepositions

next to	It's next to the bank.
across from	It's across from the movie theater.
between	It's between the library and the park.
around the corner from	It's around the corner from the hospital.

There Is/There Are

Is there a laundromat in this neighborhood?
There's one window in the bedroom.
Yes, **there is.**   No, **there isn't.**

Are there any pets in the building?
There are two windows in the bedroom.
Yes, **there are.**   No, **there aren't.**

Singular/Plural

There's one bedroom in the apartment.

There are two bedrooms in the apartment.

Is there	a superintendent **an** elevator	in the building?

There are two	superintendents elevators	in the building.

FUNCTIONS

Inquiring about Location

Where's the *restaurant?*
Where is it?

Giving Location

It's next to *the bank.*
It's across from *the movie theater.*
It's between *the library* and *the park.*
It's around the corner from *the hospital.*

There's a *laundromat* on *Main Street,* next to
   the supermarket.

Attracting Attention

Excuse me.

Checking Understanding

Two bedrooms?
   Yes. That's right.

Asking for and Reporting Information

Is there *a laundromat* in *this
   neighborhood?*
Is there a *laundromat* nearby?
   Yes. There's a *laundromat* on *Main
      Street.*

Is there a *stove* in *the kitchen?*
   Yes, there is.
   No, there isn't.
Are there any *mice* in *the basement?*
   Yes, there are.
   No, there aren't.

How many *bedrooms* are there in *the
   apartment?*
   There are *two bedrooms* in *the
      apartment.*

Tell me, _____?

Singular/Plural ■
Adjectives ■
This/That/These/Those ■

Clothing

Practice saying these words and then write them in the chart on the next page.

- hat
- shirt
- tie
- jacket
- watch
- belt
- pants
- sock
- shoe

- earring
- necklace
- blouse
- bracelet
- skirt
- stocking

- coat
- glove
- purse
- dress
- glasses
- suit
- raincoat
- umbrella
- briefcase
- sweater
- mitten
- boot

SINGULAR/PLURAL *

[s]	[z]	[ɪz]
a book – books	a car – cars	a class – classes
a shop – shops	a school – schools	a church – churches
a student – students	a window – windows	a garage – garages
a bank – banks	a store – stores	an exercise – exercises
an airport – airports	an island – islands	an office – offices

[s]	[z]	[ɪz]
a hat - hats	a skirt - skirts	a sweater - sweaters
a shirt - shirts	a stocking - stockings	a mitten - mittens
a tie - ties	a coat - coats	a boot - boots
a jacket - jackets	a glove - gloves	
a watch - watches	a purse - purses	
a belt - belts	a dress - dresses	
a pants - pants	a glasses - glasses	
a sock - socks	a suit - suits	
a shoe - shoes	a raincoat - raincots.	
a earring - earrings	a umbrella - umbrellas	
a necklace necklaces	a briefcase - briefcases	
a blouse - blouses		
a bracelet - bracelets		

*Some words have irregular plurals:
- a man – men
- a woman – women
- a child – children
- a person – people
- a tooth – teeth
- a mouse – mice

I'm Looking for a Jacket

COLORS

red   orange   yellow   green   blue   purple   black   silver

pink   gray   white   gold   brown

A. May I help you?

B. Yes, please. I'm looking for a jacket.

A. Here's a nice jacket.

B. But this is a PURPLE jacket!

A. That's okay. Purple jackets are very POPULAR this year.

A. May I help you?

B. Yes, please. I'm looking for a _____.

A. Here's a nice _____.

B. But this is a _____ _____!

A. That's okay. _____ _____s are very POPULAR this year.

1. *green*

2. *orange*

3. *red*

4. *yellow*

5. *purple*

6. *pink and green*

7. *polka dot*

8. *striped*

I'm Looking for a Pair of Gloves

pair of shoes/socks. . . .

A. Can I help you?

B. Yes, please. I'm looking for a pair of gloves.

A. Here's a nice pair of gloves.

B. But these are GREEN gloves!

A. That's okay. Green gloves are very POPULAR this year.

A. Can I help you?

B. Yes, please. I'm looking for a pair of _____.

A. Here's a nice pair of _____.

B. But these are _____ _____s!

A. That's okay. _____ _____s are very POPULAR this year.

---

1. *pink*

2. *black*

3. *red*

4. *striped*

5. *green and yellow*

6. *purple and brown*

7. *polka dot*

8. *red, white, and blue*

How about YOU?

What are you wearing today?
What are the students in your class wearing today?
What's your favorite color?

NOTHING TO WEAR

Fred is upset this morning. He's looking for something to wear to work, but there's nothing in his closet.

He's looking for a clean shirt, but all his shirts are dirty. He's looking for a sports jacket, but all his sports jackets are at the dry cleaner's. He's looking for a pair of pants, but all the pants in his closet are ripped. And he's looking for a pair of socks, but all his socks are on the clothesline, and it's raining!

Fred is having a difficult time this morning. He's getting dressed for work, but his closet is empty and there's nothing to wear.

CHECK-UP

Choose

1. Fred's closet is
   a. upset.
   b. empty.

2. Fred is
   a. at home.
   b. at work.

3. Fred's shirts are
   a. dirty.
   b. clean.

4. He's looking for a pair of
   a. jackets.
   b. pants.

5. The weather is
   a. not very good.
   b. beautiful.

6. Fred is upset because
   a. he's getting dressed.
   b. there's nothing to wear.

Choose

What word *doesn't* belong?

1. a. shoes	b. socks	c. earrings	d. boots
2. a. necklace	b. bracelet	c. sweater	d. earring
3. a. skirt	b. raincoat	c. jacket	d. coat
4. a. dress	b. blouse	c. skirt	d. tie
5. a. umbrella	b. shirt	c. briefcase	d. purse

Excuse Me. I Think That's My Jacket.

This/That is — These/Those are

1. pen
2. pencils
3. book
4. mittens
5. raincoat
6. earrings
7. sweater
8.

Lost and Found

A. Is this your umbrella?

B. No, it isn't.

A. Are you sure?

B. Yes. THAT umbrella is brown, and MY umbrella is black.

A. Are these your boots?

B. No, they aren't.

A. Are you sure?

B. Yes. THOSE boots are dirty, and MY boots are clean.

Make up conversations, using colors and other adjectives you know.

1. *watch*

2. *glasses*

3. *purse*

4. *gloves*

5. *little boy*

6. _____

CHRISTMAS SHOPPING

Mrs. Johnson is doing her Christmas shopping. She's looking for Christmas gifts for her family, but she's having a lot of trouble.

She's looking for a brown briefcase for her husband, but all the briefcases are black. She's looking for a plain tie for her brother, but all the ties are striped. She's looking for a cotton blouse for her daughter, but all the blouses are polyester.

She's looking for an inexpensive necklace for her sister, but all the necklaces are expensive. She's looking for a gray or brown raincoat for her father-in-law, but all the raincoats are yellow. And she's looking for a leather purse for her mother-in-law, but all the purses are vinyl.

Poor Mrs. Johnson is very frustrated. She's looking for special gifts for all the special people in her family, but she's having a lot of trouble.

Good luck with your Christmas shopping, Mrs. Johnson! And Merry Christmas!

✔ CHECK-UP

Q & A

Mrs. Johnson is in the department store. Using this model, create dialogs based on the story.

A. Excuse me. I'm looking for *a brown briefcase* for *my husband*.
B. I'm sorry. All our *briefcases* are *black*.

Listening

Listen and choose the word you hear.

1. a. tie   b. ties
2. a. jacket   b. jackets
3. a. blouse   b. blouses
4. a. sock   b. socks
5. a. boot   b. boots
6. a. umbrella   b. umbrellas

CHAPTER 8 *SUMMARY*

GRAMMAR

Singular/Plural

[s]
> I'm looking for **a** jacket.
> Purple jacket**s** are very popular this year.

[z]
> I'm looking for **an** umbrella.
> Purple umbrella**s** are very popular this year.

[ɪz]
> I'm looking for **a** dress.
> Pink dress**es** are very popular this year.

I'm looking for	a	jacket. hat. blouse.
	a pair of	gloves. pants. shoes.

This/That/These/Those

> Is this your umbrella?
> That umbrella is brown.

> Are these your boots?
> Those boots are dirty.

Adjectives

> This is a purple jacket.
> These are green gloves.

FUNCTIONS

Offering to Help

May I help you?
Can I help you?
  Yes, please.

Expressing Want-Desire

I'm looking for *a jacket.*

I'm looking for *a brown briefcase* for *my husband.*

Describing

Here's a nice *jacket.*

But this is a *PURPLE jacket!*
But these are *GREEN gloves!*

That *umbrella* is *brown.*
Those *boots* are *dirty.*

Expressing Agreement

You're right.

Expressing Disagreement

I don't think so.

Asking for and Reporting Information

Is this your *umbrella?*
  No, it isn't.
Are these your *boots?*
  No, they aren't.

Inquiring about Certainty

Are you sure?

Expressing Certainty

I think *that's my jacket.*

Apologizing

I'm sorry.

Admitting an Error

I guess I made a mistake.

Attracting Attention

Excuse me.

Expressing Surprise-Disbelief

But this is a PURPLE jacket!

Simple Present Tense ■

Interviews Around the World

| I
We
You
They } live. | Where do { I
we
you
they } live? | What do { I
we
you
they } do? |

A. What's your name?

B. My name is Antonio.

A. Where do you live?

B. I live in Rome.

A. What language do you speak?

B. I speak Italian.

A. Tell me, what do you do every day?

B. I eat Italian food,
I drink Italian wine,*
and I sing Italian songs!

*Or: coffee, tea, beer, etc.

Interview these people.

> What's your name?
> Where do you live?
> What language do you speak?
> What do you do every day?

1. PARIS — French — Marie

2. MADRID — Spanish — Carlos

3. BERLIN — German — Frieda

4. TOKYO — Japanese — Toshi

5. LONDON — English — Sara and Mark

6. MOSCOW — Russian — Boris and Natasha

People Around the World

| He She It } lives. | Where does { he she it } live? | What does { he she it } do? |

A. What's his name?

B. His name is Miguel.

A. Where does he live?

B. He lives in Mexico City.

A. What language does he speak?

B. He speaks Spanish.

A. What does he do every day?

B. He eats Mexican food,
he reads Mexican newspapers,
and he listens to Mexican music.

Ask and answer questions about these people.

What's his/her name?
Where does he/she live?
What language does he/she speak?
What does he/she do every day?

1.

2.

3.

4.

5.

6.

ON YOUR OWN: A Famous Person

I We You They } live. He She It } lives.	Where	*donde* do { I we you they } *donde* does { he she it } live?	What	*que hay* *Que* do { I we you they } *Que hace* *Que* does { he she it } do?

Interview a famous person.

A. What's your name?

B. My name is Lucia Méndez.

A. Where do you ~~live~~ live?

B. I lives in Mexico Cyt.

A. What language does he speak?

B. I speak spanish.

A. what do you do every day?

B. I eats enchiladas and Mole verde.

Now tell the class about this person.

His / Her name is . . .

74

MR. AND MRS. DiCARLO

Mr. and Mrs. DiCarlo live in an old Italian neighborhood in New York City. They speak a little English, but usually they speak Italian.

They read the Italian newspaper. They listen to Italian radio programs. They shop at the Italian grocery store around the corner from their apartment building. And every day they visit their friends and neighbors and talk about life back in "the old country."

Mr. and Mrs. DiCarlo are upset about their son, Joe. He lives in a small suburb outside the city, and he speaks very little Italian. He reads American newspapers. He listens to American radio programs. He shops at big suburban supermarkets and shopping malls. And when he visits his friends and neighbors, he speaks only English.

In fact, the only time Joe speaks Italian is when he calls Mr. and Mrs. DiCarlo on the telephone or when he visits every weekend.

Mr. and Mrs. DiCarlo are sad because their son speaks so little Italian. They're afraid he's forgetting his language, his culture, and his country.

CHECK-UP

Answer These Questions

1. Where do Mr. and Mrs. DiCarlo live?
2. Where does Joe live?
3. How much English do Mr. and Mrs. DiCarlo speak?
4. How much Italian does Joe speak?
5. What do Mr. and Mrs. DiCarlo read?
6. What does Joe read?
7. What do Mr. and Mrs. DiCarlo listen to?
8. What does Joe listen to?
9. Where do Mr. and Mrs. DiCarlo shop?
10. Where does Joe shop?

What's the Word?

1. Mr. DiCarlo _____ a little English.
2. Mrs. DiCarlo _____ at the grocery store.
3. They _____ the Italian newspaper every day.
4. Joe _____ outside the city.
5. He _____ American radio programs.
6. His friends _____ only English.
7. Mrs. DiCarlo _____ her neighbors every day.
8. She _____ about life in "the old country."
9. Their friends _____ in New York City.
10. They _____ their friends on the telephone.

Choose

What word *doesn't* belong?

1. a. coffee	b. newspaper	c. tea	d. wine
2. a. French	b. Spanish	c. Rome	d. German
3. a. Italian	b. Russian	c. Japanese	d. New York
4. a. mall	b. supermarket	c. neighborhood	d. store
5. a. son	b. friend	c. neighbor	d. landlord
6. a. lunch	b. dinner	c. food	d. restaurant

Listening

Listen and choose the best answer.

1. a. The newspaper.	b. Mexican food.
2. a. The newspaper.	b. Mexican food.
3. a. Their clothes.	b. TV.
4. a. Their clothes.	b. TV.
5. a. Songs.	b. Coffee.
6. a. Songs.	b. Coffee.

IN YOUR OWN WORDS

For Writing and Discussion

MRS. KOWALSKI

Mrs. Kowalski lives in an old Polish neighborhood in Chicago. She's upset about her son, Michael, and his wife, Kathy. Using the story on page 75 as a model, tell a story about Mrs. Kowalski.

Tell about yourself:
    What do you do every day?
    Who do you visit?
    What do you talk about?

Now, tell about another person (a friend, someone in your family, or another student in your class):
    What does he/she do every day?
    Who does he/she visit?
    What does he/she talk about?

GRAMMAR

Simple Present Tense

Where	do	I we you they	live?
	does	he she it	

I We You They	live	in Rome.
He She It	lives	

FUNCTIONS

Asking for and Reporting Information

What's your name?
  My name is *Antonio*.
Where do you live?
  I live in *Rome*.
What language do you speak?
  I speak *Italian*.
What do you do every day?
  I *eat Italian food*.

Tell me, _____?

Simple Present Tense:
Yes/No Questions ■
Negatives ■
Short Answers ■

Stanley's International Restaurant

He cooks. He doesn't cook. (does not)	Does he cook? Yes, he does. No, he doesn't.	When What kind of food } does he cook?

Stanley's International Restaurant is a very special place. Every day Stanley cooks a different kind of food. On Monday he cooks Italian food. On Tuesday he cooks Greek food. On Wednesday he cooks Chinese food. On Thursday he cooks Puerto Rican food. On Friday he cooks Japanese food. On Saturday he cooks Mexican food. And on Sunday he cooks American food.

Ask and answer six questions based on this model.

A. What kind of food does Stanley cook **on Monday**?

B. **On Monday** he cooks **Italian** food.

Ask six questions with "yes" answers based on this model.

A. Does Stanley cook **Greek** food on **Tuesday**?

B. Yes, he does.

Ask six questions with "no" answers based on this model.

A. Does Stanley cook **Japanese** food on **Sunday**?

B. No, he doesn't.

A. When does he cook **Japanese** food?

B. He cooks **Japanese** food on **Friday**.

A. Do you go to Stanley's Restaurant on **Wednesday**?
B. Yes, I do.
A. Why?
B. Because I like **Chinese** food.

Ask these people.

1. *Friday?*

2. *Saturday?*

3. *Monday?*

4. *Thursday?*

A. Do you go to Stanley's Restaurant on **Sunday**?
B. No, I don't.
A. Why not?
B. Because I don't like **American** food.

Ask these people.

5. *Monday?*

6. *Tuesday?*

7. *Wednesday?*

8. *Saturday?*

A. What kind of food do you like?
B. I like **Russian** food.
A. When do you go to Stanley's Restaurant?
B. I don't go there.
A. Why not?
B. Because Stanley doesn't cook **Russian** food.

Ask these people.

9. *Vietnamese*

10. *Ethiopian*

11. *Thai*

12. *Hungarian*

81

A. What do people do at Stanley's International Restaurant?

B. On Monday they speak Italian, eat Italian food, drink Italian wine, and listen to Italian music.

1. Henry likes Greek food.

   When does he go to Stanley's Restaurant?
   What does he do there?

2. Alice likes Mexican food.

   When does she go to Stanley's Restaurant?
   What does she do there?

3. Mr. and Mrs. Wilson go to Stanley's Restaurant on Wednesday.

   What kind of food do they like?
   What do they do there?

4. What kind of food do YOU like?
   When do you go to Stanley's Restaurant?
   What do you do there?

CLASSROOM DRAMA: You Speak English Very Well

$$\text{Yes,} \begin{Bmatrix} \text{I} \\ \text{we} \\ \text{you} \\ \text{they} \end{Bmatrix} \text{do.} \qquad \begin{Bmatrix} \text{he} \\ \text{she} \\ \text{it} \end{Bmatrix} \text{does.}$$

$$\text{No,} \begin{Bmatrix} \text{I} \\ \text{we} \\ \text{you} \\ \text{they} \end{Bmatrix} \text{don't.} \qquad \begin{Bmatrix} \text{he} \\ \text{she} \\ \text{it} \end{Bmatrix} \text{doesn't.}$$

Act this out in class.

EVERY WEEKEND IS IMPORTANT TO THE FRANKLIN FAMILY

Every weekend is important to the Franklin family. During the week they don't have very much time together, but they spend A LOT of time together on the weekend.

Mr. Franklin works at the shoe store downtown during the week, but he doesn't work there on the weekend. Mrs. Franklin works at the city hospital during the week, but she doesn't work there on the weekend. Bobby and Sally Franklin go to the elementary school during the week, but they don't go there on the weekend. And the Franklin's dog, Rover, stays home alone during the week, but he doesn't stay home alone on the weekend.

On Saturday and Sunday the Franklins spend their time together. On Saturday morning they clean the house together. On Saturday afternoon they work in the garden together. And on Saturday evening they sit in the living room and watch TV together. On Sunday morning they go to church together. On Sunday afternoon they have a big dinner together. And on Sunday evening they play their musical instruments together.

As you can see, every weekend is special to the Franklins. It's their only time together as a family.

Q & A

Using these models, make questions and answers based on the story on page 84.

A. What *does Mr. Franklin* do during the week?

B. *He works at the shoe store downtown.*

A. What do the Franklins do on *Saturday morning?*

B. They *clean the house* together.

Do or Does?

1. What kind of food _____ you like?
2. _____ Mr. Franklin go to Stanley's Restaurant?
3. _____ you speak Spanish?
4. When _____ Bobby go to school?
5. _____ she work downtown?
6. Where _____ they live?

Listening
Choose the best answer to finish the sentence.

1. a. you do.   b. they do.
2. a. he does.   b. he doesn't.
3. a. I do.   b. he does.
4. a. she does.   b. we do.
5. a. they don't.   b. we don't.
6. a. she does.   b. she doesn't.
7. a. I do.   b. I don't.
8. a. he doesn't.   b. she doesn't.

Answer These Questions

1. Does Mr. Franklin work at the shoe store?
2. Do Bobby and Sally go to school during the week?
3. Does Mrs. Franklin work at the shoe store?
4. Do Mr. and Mrs. Franklin have much time together during the week?
5. Does Sally Franklin watch TV on Saturday evening?
6. Do Sally and her brother clean the house on Saturday morning?
7. Does Mr. Franklin work in the garden on Saturday evening?

Don't or Doesn't?

1. My husband _____ like international food.
2. I _____ like coffee.
3. They _____ play musical instruments.
4. Mrs. Wilson _____ shop at the mall.
5. My sister and I _____ watch TV during the week.
6. Our dog _____ like our neighbor's cat.

A VERY OUTGOING PERSON

Alice is a very outgoing person. She spends a lot of time with her friends. She goes to parties. She goes to movies. And she goes to night clubs. She's very popular.

She also likes sports very much. She plays basketball. She plays baseball. And she plays volleyball. She's very athletic.

Alice doesn't stay home alone very often. She doesn't read many books. She doesn't watch TV. And she doesn't listen to music. She's very active.

As you can see, Alice is a very outgoing person.

IN YOUR OWN WORDS

For Writing and Discussion

A VERY SHY PERSON

Using the story about Alice as a model, tell a story about Sheldon. Begin your story:

Sheldon is a very shy person. He doesn't spend a lot of time with his friends. He doesn't go . . .

How about YOU?

Tell about yourself:
What kind of person are you?
Are you outgoing? Are you shy?
Tell how you spend your time.

ON YOUR OWN: Who Is Your Favorite . . . ?

Answer these questions and then ask other students in your class.

1. **a.** What kind of movies do you like?
    (Do you like comedies? dramas?
    westerns? adventure movies?
    science fiction movies? cartoons?)

    b. Who is your favorite actor?
    actress?

2. **a.** What kind of books do you like?
    (Do you like novels? poetry? short
    stories?)

    b. Who is your favorite author?

3. **a.** What kind of TV programs do you
    like?
    (Do you like comedies? dramas?
    cartoons? game shows? news
    programs?)

    b. Who is your favorite TV star?

4. What's your favorite food?

5. **a.** What kind of music do you like?
    (Do you like classical music?
    popular music? jazz? rock music?)

    b. Who is your favorite singer?
    (What kind of songs does he/she
    sing?)

6. **a.** Which sports do you like?
    (Do you like football? baseball?
    soccer? golf? hockey? tennis?)

    b. Who is your favorite athlete?

87

GRAMMAR

Simple Present Tense: Yes/No Questions

Do	I we you they	go to Stanley's Restaurant?
Does	he she it	

Short Answers

Yes,	I we you they	do.
	he she it	does.

No,	I we you they	don't.
	he she it	doesn't.

Simple Present Tense: Negatives

I We You They	don't	like American food.
He She It	doesn't	

FUNCTIONS

Asking for and Reporting Information

What *do you do there?*
What kind of *food does Stanley cook on Monday?*
When *does he cook Japanese food?*

Do you *go to Stanley's Restaurant?*
   Yes, I do.
   No, I don't.
Does *Stanley cook Greek food on Tuesday?*
   Yes, *he* does.
   No, *he* doesn't.

Inquiring about Likes/Dislikes

What kind of *food* do you like?
Which *sports* do you like?

Do you like *comedies?*

Who is your favorite *actor?*
What's your favorite *food?*

Expressing Likes

I like *Chinese food.*

Expressing Dislikes

I don't like *American food.*

Complimenting

You *speak English* very well.

Object Pronouns ▪
Simple Present Tense:
  s vs. non-s Endings ▪
Have/Has ▪
Adverbs of Frequency ▪

How Often?

I	me
he	him
she	her
it	it
we	us
you	you
they	them

A. How often does your boyfriend call you?

B. He calls me every night.

1. How often do you speak to your daughter?

   every day

3. How often do you paint your house?

   every year

5. How often do your grandchildren visit you?

   every Sunday

7. How often does your boss say "hello" to you?

   every day

2. How often do you write to your son at college?

   every week

4. How often do you clean your windows?

   every month

6. How often do you wash your car?

   every weekend

8. How often do you think about me?

   all the time

She Usually Studies in the Library

[s]		[z]		[ɪz]			
eat	eats	read	reads	wash	washes	always	100%
write	writes	bring	brings	watch	watches	usually	90%
bark	barks	call	calls	dance	dances	sometimes	50%
speak	speaks	clean	cleans	fix	fixes	rarely	10%
						never	0%

A. Does Carmen usually study in her room?

B. No. She rarely studies in her room. She usually studies in the library.

1. Does Sally usually eat lunch in the cafeteria?

   rarely

   outside

2. Does Andrew always watch the news after dinner?

   never

   game shows

3. Does Irene always read *The National Inquirer?*

   never

   Time magazine

4. Does Henry usually wash his car on Saturday?

   rarely

   on Sunday

5. Does your boyfriend sometimes bring you flowers?

   never

   candy

6. Does your neighbor's dog always bark at night?

   never

   during the day

We Have Noisy Neighbors

I
We
You
They
} have

brown eyes

He
She
It
} has

A. Do you have quiet neighbors?

B. No. We have noisy neighbors.

1. Do you have a cat?
   a dog

2. Do Mr. and Mrs. Hill have a new car?
   an old car

3. Does this store have an elevator?
   an escalator

4. Do you have a brother?
   a sister

5. Does your daughter have straight hair?
   curly hair

6. Does your baby boy have blue eyes?
   brown eyes

My brother and I look very different. I have brown eyes and he has blue eyes. We both have brown hair, but I have short, curly hair and he has long, straight hair. I'm tall and thin. He's short and heavy.

As you can see, I don't look like my brother. We look very different.

Who in your family do you look like? Who DON'T you look like? Explain.

My sister and I are very different. I'm a teacher. She's a journalist. I live in Chicago. She lives in Paris. I have a small house in the suburbs. She has a large apartment in the city.

I'm married. She's single. I play golf. She plays tennis. I play the piano. She doesn't play a musical instrument. On the weekend I usually watch TV and rarely go out. She never watches TV and always goes to parties.

As you can see, we're very different. But we're sisters . . . and we're friends.

Compare yourself with a member of your family, another student in your class, or a famous person. Explain how you and this person are different.

CLOSE FRIENDS

My husband and I are very lucky. We have many close friends in this city, and they're all interesting people.

Our friend Greta is an actress. We see her when she isn't making a movie in Hollywood. When we get together with her, she always tells us about her life in Hollywood as a movie star. Greta is a very close friend. We like her very much.

Our friend Dan is a scientist. We see him when he isn't busy in his laboratory. When we get together with him, he always tells us about his new experiments. Dan is a very close friend. We like him very much.

Our friends Bob and Carol are famous newspaper reporters. We see them when they aren't traveling around the world. When we get together with them, they always tell us about their conversations with presidents and prime ministers. Bob and Carol are very close friends. We like them very much.

Unfortunately, we don't see Greta, Dan, Bob, and Carol very often. In fact, we rarely see them because they're usually so busy. But we think about them all the time.

What's the Word?

Dan is always busy. _____ works in _____ laboratory every day. Dan's friends rarely see
1   2

_____. When they see _____, _____ usually talks about _____ experiments. Everybody
3   4   5   6

likes _____ very much. _____ is a very nice person.
7   8

Greta is a famous actress. _____ lives in Hollywood. _____ movies are very popular.
9   10

When _____ walks down the street, people always say "hello" to _____ and tell _____ how
11   12   13

much they like _____ movies.
14

Bob and Carol are reporters. _____ friends don't see _____ very often because _____
15   16   17

travel around the world all the time. Presidents and prime ministers often call _____ on the
18

telephone. _____ like _____ work very much.
19   20

Listening

Who and what are they talking about?

1. a. daughter
    b. son

2. a. window
    b. windows

3. a. grandfather
    b. aunt

4. a. sink
    b. toilets

5. a. Mr. Jones
    b. Mr. and Mrs. Jones

6. a. Mr. Green
    b. Mr. and Mrs. Green

IN YOUR OWN WORDS

For Writing and Discussion

MY CLOSE FRIENDS

Tell about your close friends.

What are their names?
Where do they live?
What do they do?
When do you get together with them?
What do you talk about?

GRAMMAR

Object Pronouns

He calls	me him her it us you them	every night.

Have/Has

I We You They	have	brown eyes.
He She It	has	

Simple Present Tense: s vs. non-s Endings

I We You They	eat. read. wash.

Adverbs of Frequency

I	always usually sometimes rarely never	wash my car.

He She It	eats. reads. washes.	[s] [z] [ɪz]

FUNCTIONS

Asking for and Reporting Information

How often *does your boyfriend call you?*
  He calls me every night.

Does *Carmen* usually *study in her room?*
  No. *She* rarely *studies in her room.*
  She usually *studies in the library.*

Do you have *quiet neighbors?*

I'm a *teacher.*
I live in *Chicago.*
I have *a small house.*
I'm *married.*
I play *golf.*
I play *the piano.*
I usually *watch* TV and rarely *go out.*

Describing

We have noisy neighbors.
They have an old car.

My brother and I look very different.
I don't look like *my brother.*

My sister and I are very different.

I have *brown* eyes.
He has *blue* eyes.

I have *short, curly* hair.
He has *long, straight* hair.

I'm *tall* and *thin.*
He's *short* and *heavy.*

Contrast:
Simple Present and
Present Continuous
Tenses ■
Adjectives ■

I Always Cry When I'm Sad

Why are you crying?

I'm crying because I'm sad.
I ALWAYS cry when I'm sad.

1. Why are you smiling?

_____ happy.

I ALWAYS _____.

2. Why is he shouting?

_____ angry.

He ALWAYS _____.

3. Why is she biting her nails?

_____ nervous.

She ALWAYS _____.

4. Why is the bird drinking?

_____ thirsty.

It ALWAYS _____.

5. Why are they going to Stanley's Restaurant?

_____ hungry.

They ALWAYS _____.

6. Why is he going to the doctor?

_____ sick.

He ALWAYS _____.

7. Why are they shivering?

_____ cold.

They ALWAYS _____.

8. Why are you perspiring?

_____ hot.

I ALWAYS _____.

9. Why is she yawning?

_____ tired.

She ALWAYS _____.

10. Why is he blushing?

_____ embarrassed.

He ALWAYS _____.

ON YOUR OWN: What Do You Do When You're Nervous?

What do you do when you're nervous?

Do you perspire?

Do you bite your nails?

Do you walk back and forth?

Answer these questions and then ask another student in your class.

What do you do when you're . . .

1. nervous?

   When I'm nervous I bite my nails.
   _____

2. sad?

   _____

3. happy?

   _____

4. tired?

   _____

5. sick?

   _____

6. cold?

   _____

7. hot?

   _____

8. hungry?

   _____

9. thirsty?

   _____

10. angry?

    _____

11. embarrassed?

    _____

I'm Washing the Dishes in the Bathtub

A. What are you doing?!

B. I'm washing the dishes in the bathtub.

A. That's strange! Do you USUALLY wash the dishes in the bathtub?

B. No. I NEVER wash the dishes in the bathtub, but I'm washing the dishes in the bathtub TODAY.

A. Why are you doing THAT?!

B. Because my sink is broken.

A. I'm sorry to hear that.

A. What are you doing?!

B. I'm _____.

A. That's strange! Do you USUALLY _____?

B. No. I NEVER _____, but I'm _____ TODAY.

A. Why are you doing THAT?!

B. Because my _____ is broken.

A. I'm sorry to hear that.

1. *sleep*
   sleeping } *on the floor*
   bed

2. *cook*
   cooking } *on the radiator*
   stove

3. *study*
   studying } *English by candlelight*
   lamp

4. *shout*
   shouting } *to my neighbor across*
   the street

   telephone

5. *hitchhike*
   hitchhiking } *to work*
   car

6.

A BAD DAY AT THE OFFICE

Mr. Blaine is the president of the Acme Insurance Company. His company is very large and always very busy. Mr. Blaine has a staff of energetic employees who work for him. Unfortunately, all of his employees are out today. Nobody is there. As a result, Mr. Blaine is doing everybody's job, and he's having a VERY bad day at the office!

He's answering the telephone because the receptionist who usually answers it is at the dentist's office. He's typing letters because the secretary who usually types them is at home in bed with the flu. He's operating the computer because the computer programmer who usually operates it is on vacation. He's even fixing the radiator because the custodian who usually fixes it is on strike.

Poor Mr. Blaine! It's a very busy day at the Acme Insurance Company, and nobody is there to help him. He's having a VERY bad day at the office!

CHECK-UP

True or False?

1. Mr. Blaine is the president of the Ajax Insurance Company.
2. Mr. Blaine is out today.
3. The secretary is sick.
4. The computer programmer is on strike.
5. Mr. Blaine's receptionist usually answers the phone at the dentist's office.

Listening

Listen and choose the best answer.

1. a. I wash dishes.
   b. I'm washing dishes.

2. a. He types.
   b. He's typing.

3. a. She answers the telephone.
   b. She's answering the telephone.

4. a. Yes. He shouts.
   b. Yes. He's shouting.

5. a. I call the doctor.
   b. I'm calling the doctor.

EARLY MONDAY MORNING IN CENTERVILLE

    Early Monday morning is usually a very busy time in Centerville. Men and women usually rush to their jobs. Some people walk to work, some people drive, and others take the bus. Children usually go to school. Some children walk to school, some children take the school bus, and others ride their bicycles. The city is usually very busy. Trucks deliver food to the supermarkets, mail carriers deliver mail to homes and businesses, and police officers direct traffic at every corner. Yes, early Monday morning is usually a very busy time in Centerville.

✔ CHECK-UP

Using the story above as a guide, complete the following:

THE SNOWSTORM

    Today isn't a typical early Monday morning in Centerville. In fact, it's a very unusual morning. It's snowing very hard there. All the people are at home. The streets are empty and the city is quiet. The men and women who usually rush to their jobs aren't rushing to their jobs today. The people who usually walk to work aren't walking, the people who usually drive aren't _____, and the people who usually take the bus aren't _____ the bus. The children who usually go to school aren't _____ to school today. The children who usually _____ aren't _____. The children who usually _____ the school bus aren't _____ it today. And the children who usually _____ their bicycles aren't _____ them this morning.

    The city is very quiet. The trucks that usually _____ aren't _____ today. The mail carriers who usually _____ aren't _____ this morning. And the police officers who usually _____ aren't _____ today. Yes, it's a very unusual Monday morning in Centerville.

CHAPTER 12   *SUMMARY*

GRAMMAR

Simple Present Tense

I always **cry** when I'm sad.
I never **wash** the dishes in the bathtub.

Present Continuous Tense

I'm crying because I'm sad.
I'm washing the dishes in the bathtub today.

Adjectives

I'm	angry. cold. embarrassed. happy.	hot. hungry. nervous. sad.	sick. thirsty. tired.

FUNCTIONS

Asking for and Reporting Information

Why *are you crying?*
   I'm crying because *I'm sad.*

What are you doing?
   I'm *washing the dishes in the bathtub.*

Do you usually *wash the dishes in the
   bathtub?*

My *sink* is broken.

Describing Feelings-Emotions

I'm *angry/cold/embarrassed/happy/hot/
   hungry/nervous/sad/sick/thirsty/tired.*

When I'm *nervous* I *bite my nails.*

Expressing Surprise-Disbelief

That's strange!

Sympathizing

I'm sorry to hear that.

Can ▪

Have to ▪

Can You?

I
He
She
It
We
You
They
} can/can't (cannot) sing.

Can you sing?
Yes, I can.
No, I can't.

1. Can Mary ski? 2. Can Sam cook Chinese food?

3. Can they play the violin? 4. Can you sing?

5. Can Jeff play chess? 6. Can William play the piano?

7. Can Sally play football? 8. Can they skate?

9. Ask another student in your class: Can you _____?

Of Course They Can

A. Can Jack fix cars?

B. Of course he can.
He fixes cars every day. He's a mechanic.

1. Can Arthur play the violin?
violinist

2. Can Anita sing?
singer

3. Can Fred and Ginger dance?
dancer

4. Can Stanley cook?
chef

5. Can Lois bake apple pies?
baker

6. Can Richard act?
actor

7. Can Elizabeth and Katherine act?
actress

8. Can Eleanor teach?
teacher

9. Can Shirley drive a truck?
truck driver

107

THE ACE EMPLOYMENT SERVICE

Roy, Susan, Lana, and Tina are sitting in the reception room at the Ace Employment Service. They're all looking for work, and they're hoping they can find jobs today.

Roy is looking for a job as a superintendent. He can paint walls. He can fix motors. And he can repair locks. Susan is looking for a job as a secretary. She can type. She can file. And she can speak well on the telephone. Lana and Tina are looking for jobs as actresses. They can sing. They can dance. And they can act.

Good luck, Roy! Good luck, Susan! Good luck, Lana and Tina! We hope you can find the jobs you're looking for.

Q & A

Roy, Susan, Lana, and Tina are having their interviews at the Ace Employment Service. Using this model, create dialogs based on the story.

A. What's your name?
B. *Roy Smith.*
A. Nice to meet you. Tell me, *Roy,* what kind of job are you looking for?
B. I'm looking for a job as a *superintendent.*
A. What can you do?
B. I can *paint walls, fix motors,* and *repair locks.*

Listening

Can or Can't?

Listen and circle.

1. a. can   b. can't
2. a. can   b. can't
3. a. can   b. can't
4. a. can   b. can't
5. a. can   b. can't
6. a. can   b. can't

What Can They Do?

Choose what each person can do.

1. a. sing   b. dance
2. a. file   b. type
3. a. fix motors   b. repair locks
4. a. cook   b. bake
5. a. drive a truck   b. drive a bus
6. a. teach history   b. teach science

They Can't Go to Herbert's Party

I We You They	have to	
		work.
He She It	has to	

Herbert is depressed. He's having a party today, but his friends can't go to his party. They're all busy.

A. Can Michael go to Herbert's party?

B. No, he can't. He has to go to the doctor.

1. *Peggy?*
   fix her car

2. *George and Martha?*
   go to the supermarket

3. *Nancy?*
   go to the dentist

4. *Henry?*
   clean his apartment

5. *Carl and Tim?*
   do their homework

6. *Linda?*
   wash her clothes

7. *Ted?*
   go to the bank

8. Can YOU go to Herbert's party?
   No, _____.

APPLYING FOR A DRIVER'S LICENSE

Henry is annoyed. He's applying for a driver's license, and he's upset about all the things he has to do.

First, he has to go to the Motor Vehicles Department and pick up an application form. He can't ask for the form by telephone, and he can't ask for it by mail. He has to go downtown and pick up the form in person.

He has to fill out the form in duplicate. He can't use a pencil. He has to use a pen. He can't use blue ink. He has to use black ink. And he can't write in script. He has to print.

He also has to attach two photographs to the application. They can't be old photographs. They have to be new. They can't be large. They have to be small. And they can't be black and white. They have to be color.

Then he has to submit his application. He has to wait in a long line to pay his application fee. He has to wait in another long line to have an eye examination. And believe it or not, he has to wait in ANOTHER long line to take a written test!

Finally, he has to take a road test. He has to start the car. He has to make a right turn, a left turn, and a U-turn. And he even has to park his car on a crowded city street.

No wonder Henry is annoyed! He's applying for his driver's license, and he can't believe all the things he has to do.

CHECK-UP

Answer These Questions

1. Can Henry apply for a driver's license by mail?
2. Where does he have to go to apply for a license?
3. How many photographs does he have to attach to the application?
4. Can Henry use black and white photographs?
5. What does he have to do during the road test?

Fix This Sign

This sign at the Motor Vehicles Department is wrong. The things people have to do are in the wrong order. On a separate sheet of paper, fix the sign based on the story.

How to Apply for a Driver's License

Have an eye examination.
Pay the application fee.
Take a road test.
Pick up an application form.
Take a written test.
Fill out the form in duplicate.

IN YOUR OWN WORDS

For Writing and Discussion

Explain how to apply for one of the following: a passport, a marriage license, a loan, or something else. In your explanation, use "You have to."*

*"You have to" = "A person has to"

Make up conversations with other students in your class.

Include some of these words in your questions.

go to a movie
go to a baseball game
have lunch
have dinner
go swimming
go dancing
go skating
go skiing
go shopping
go bowling
go sailing
go jogging

Include some of these words and others in your answers.

go to the doctor
go to the bank
do my homework
visit a friend in the hospital
work

_____
_____
_____
_____
_____
_____
_____

GRAMMAR

Can

Can	I he she it we you they	sing?

I He She It We You They	can can't	sing.

Have to

I We You They	have to	work.
He She It	has to	

Yes,	I he she it we you they	can.

No,	I he she it we you they	can't.

FUNCTIONS

Inquiring about Ability

Can you *speak Hungarian?*
Can *Michael go to Herbert's party?*

What can you do?

Expressing Ability

I can *speak Rumanian.*

Of course *he* can.

Expressing Inability

No, I can't.

Asking for and Reporting Information

He *fixes cars* every day.
He's a *mechanic.*

What's your name?
  Roy Smith.

Tell me, *Roy,* _____?

Inquiring about Want-Desire

What kind of job are you looking for?
  I'm looking for a job as a
    superintendent.

Expressing Obligation

I have to *do my laundry.*
He has to *go to the doctor.*

Extending an Invitation

Can you *go to a movie* with me on *Friday?*

Declining an Invitation

I'm sorry. I can't.

Greeting People

Nice to meet you.

Future: Going to ■
Time Expressions ■
Want to ■

What Are They Going to Do Tomorrow?

(I am)	I'm	
(He is)	He's	
(She is)	She's	
(It is)	It's	} going to read.
(We are)	We're	
(You are)	You're	
(They are)	They're	

	am	I	
What	is	{ he she it }	going to do?
	are	{ we you they }	

A. What's Fred going to do tomorrow?

B. He's going to fix his car.

1. *Mary*

2. *Carol and Dan*

3. *you*

4. *Tom*

5. *you*

6. *Henry*

They're Going to the Beach

They're going to go to the beach tomorrow. = They're going to the beach tomorrow.

today	tomorrow
this morning	tomorrow morning
this afternoon	tomorrow afternoon
this evening	tomorrow evening
tonight	tomorrow night

A. What are Mr. and Mrs. Brown going to do tomorrow?

B. They're going (to go) to the beach.

1. What's Jane going to do tomorrow evening?

2. What are Ken and Barbara going to do tonight?

3. What are you going to do this afternoon?

4. What are you and your sister going to do tomorrow morning?

5. What's Ahmed going to do today?

6. What are you going to do tomorrow?

When Are You Going to . . . ?

*Other phrases you can use are:

    this/next week, month, year
    this/next Sunday, Monday, Tuesday, Wednesday, Thursday, Friday, Saturday
    this/next January, February, March, April, May, June, July, August,
                September, October, November, December
    this/next spring, summer, fall (autumn), winter

†Or: I'm going to call him right away/immediately/at once.

1. When are you going to wash your car?

2. When are you going to call your grandmother?

3. When are you going to visit us?

4. When are you going to cut your hair?

5. When are you going to plant flowers this year?

6. When are you going to fix your car?

7. When are you going to write to your Uncle John?

8. Mr. Smith! When are you going to iron those pants?

9. Ask another student: When are you going to _____?

HAPPY NEW YEAR!

It's December thirty-first, New Year's Eve. Bob and Sally Simpson are celebrating the holiday with their children, Lucy and Tom. The Simpsons are a very happy family this New Year's Eve. Next year is going to be a very good year for the entire family.

Next year, Bob and Sally are going to take a long vacation. They're going to visit Sally's cousin in California. Lucy is going to finish high school. She's going to move to Boston and begin college. Tom is going to get his driver's license. He's going to save a lot of money and buy a used car.

As you can see, the Simpsons are really looking forward to next year. It's going to be a happy year for all of them.

Happy New Year!

 CHECK-UP

Complete the Conversation

Fill in the missing words and practice the dialog with another student.

A. Lucy, _____ do next year?
    ₁

B. _____ begin college.
    ₂

A. And your brother? _____ do next year?
    ₃

B. _____ get his driver's license.
    ₄

A. How about your parents? _____ do next year?
    ₅

B. _____ take a long vacation.
    ₆

A. Well, Happy New Year, Lucy!

B. Happy New Year!

Listening

Listen and choose the words you hear.

1. a. Next month.   b. Next Monday.   6. a. This evening.   b. This morning.
2. a. This Sunday.   b. This summer.   7. a. This Tuesday.   b. This Thursday.
3. a. Tomorrow afternoon.   b. This afternoon.   8. a. Next winter.   b. Next summer.
4. a. Next November.   b. Next December.   9. a. Tomorrow.   b. This March.
5. a. Next year.   b. Next week.   10. a. This month.   b. At once.

What's the Forecast?

I We You They	} want to	
He She It	} wants to	study.

A. What are you going to do tomorrow?

B. I don't know. I want to **go swimming,** but I think the weather is going to be bad.

A. Really? What's the forecast?

B. The radio says it's going to **rain.**

A. That's strange! According to the newspaper, it's going to **be sunny.**

B. I hope you're right. I REALLY want to **go swimming.**

1. *have a picnic*
   rain
   be nice

2. *go skiing*
   be warm
   snow

3. *go to the beach*
   be cloudy
   be sunny

4. *plant flowers in my garden*
   be very hot
   be cool

5. *go sailing*
   be foggy
   be clear

6. *go to the zoo with my children*
   be cold
   be warm

Discuss in class.

What's the weather today?
What's the weather forecast for tomorrow?

What Time Is It?

It's 11:00. It's eleven o'clock.

It's 11:15. It's eleven fifteen.*

It's 11:30. It's eleven thirty.*

It's 11:45. It's eleven forty-five.*

It's 12:00. It's twelve o'clock.

It's noon. It's midnight.

*You can also say:

11:15 – a quarter after eleven
11:30 – half past eleven
11:45 – a quarter to twelve

A. What time does the movie begin?

B. It begins at 8:00.

A. At 8:00?! Oh no! We're going to be late!

B. Why? What time is it?

A. It's 7:30! We have to leave RIGHT NOW!

B. I can't leave now. I'm SHAVING!

A. Please try to hurry! I don't want to be late for the movie.

A. What time does _____?

B. It _____ at _____.

A. At _____?! Oh no! We're going to be late!

B. Why? What time is it?

A. It's _____! We have to leave RIGHT NOW!

B. I can't leave now. I'm _____!

A. Please try to hurry! I don't want to be late for the _____.

1. What time does the football game begin?
   2:00/1:30
   taking a bath

2. What time does the plane leave?
   4:15/3:45
   putting on my clothes

3. What time does English class begin?
   9:00/8:45
   getting up

4. What time does the bus leave?
   7:00/6:30
   packing my suitcase

5. What time does the train leave?
   5:15/4:30
   taking a shower

6. What time does the play begin?
   8:30/8:00
   looking for my pants

7. _____

THE FORTUNE TELLER

Walter is visiting Madame Sophia, the famous fortune teller. He's very concerned about his future, and Madame Sophia is telling him what is going to happen next year. According to Madame Sophia, next year is going to be a very interesting year in Walter's life.

In January he's going to meet a very nice woman and fall in love.

In February he's going to get married.

In March he's going to take a trip to a warm, sunny place.

In April he's going to have a bad cold.

In May his parents are going to move to a beautiful city in California.

In June there's going to be a fire in his apartment building, and he's going to have to find a new place to live.

In July his friends are going to give him a radio for his birthday.

In August his boss is going to fire him.

In September he's going to start a new job with a very big salary.

In October he's going to be in a car accident, but he isn't going to be hurt.

In November he's going to be on a television game show and win a new car.

And in December he's going to become a father!

    According to Madame Sophia, a lot is certainly going to happen in Walter's life next year. But Walter isn't sure he believes any of this. He doesn't believe in fortunes or fortune tellers. But in January he's going to get a haircut and buy a lot of new clothes, just in case Madame Sophia is right and he meets a wonderful woman and falls in love!

 *CHECK-UP*

Q & A

Walter is talking to Madame Sophia. Using these models, create dialogs based on the story.

A. Tell me, what's going to happen in *January?*
B. In *January?* Oh, . . . *January* is going to be a very good month.
A. Really? What's going to happen?
B. *You're going to meet a very nice woman and fall in love.*
A. Oh! That's wonderful!

A. Tell me, what's going to happen in *April?*
B. In *April?* Oh, . . . *April* is going to be a very bad month.
A. Really? What's going to happen?
B. *You're going to have a bad cold.*
A. Oh! That's terrible!

CHAPTER 14 *SUMMARY*

GRAMMAR

Future: Going to

What	am	I	going to do?
	is	he she it	
	are	we you they	

		going to read.
(I am)	I'm	
(He is) (She is) (It is)	He's She's It's	
(We are) (You are) (They are)	We're You're They're	

Time Expressions

I'm going to wash my clothes	today. this morning. this afternoon. this evening. tonight.	tomorrow. tomorrow morning. tomorrow afternoon. tomorrow evening. tomorrow night.	right now. right away. immediately. at once.

I'm going to fix my car	this next	week. month. year. spring. summer. fall (autumn). winter.	Sunday. Monday. Tuesday. Wednesday. Thursday. Friday. Saturday.	January. February. March. April. May. June.	July. August. September. October. November. December.

It's	11:00 (eleven o'clock.) 11:15 (eleven fifteen / a quarter after eleven.) 11:30 (eleven thirty / half past eleven.) 11:45 (eleven forty-five / a quarter to twelve.) noon. midnight.

Want to

I We You They	want to	study.
He She It	wants to	

FUNCTIONS

Inquiring about Intention

What are you going to do tomorrow?
When are you going to *wash your clothes?*

Expressing Intention

I'm going to *paint my kitchen.*
I'm going to *wash them this week.*

Expressing Want-Desire

I want to *go swimming.*
I really want to *go swimming.*

Asking for and Reporting Information

What's the forecast?
What's the weather today?
What's the weather forecast for tomorrow?
    The radio says it's going to *rain.*
    According to the newspaper, it's going to *be sunny.*

What time is it?
    It's *7:30.*

What time does the *movie* begin?
    It begins at *8:00.*

Tell me, _____?

Past Tense:
Regular Verbs ▪
Introduction to
Irregular Verbs ▪

How Do You Feel Today?

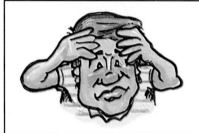

A. What's the matter?

B. I have a headache.

1. *stomachache*

2. *toothache*

3. *backache*

4. *earache*

5. *sore throat*

6. *cold*

Ask another student in your class.

A. How do you feel today?

B. _____.

A. I'm glad to hear that.

A. How do you feel today?

B. _____.

A. What's the matter?

B. I have _____.

A. I'm sorry to hear that.

What Did You Do Yesterday?

I work every day.		I work**ed** yesterday.
I play the piano every day.		I play**ed** the piano yesterday.
I rest every day.		I rest**ed** yesterday.

work	– work**ed**	[t]
play	– play**ed**	[d]
rest	– rest**ed**	[ɪd]

What did you do yesterday?

[t]

1. *I worked*

2. *cook*

3. *talk on the telephone*

4. *fix*

5. *brush*

6. *dance*

7. *wash*

8. *watch*

[d]

9. *play*

10. *study*

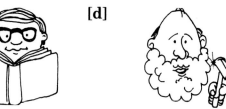

11. *shave*

12. *smile*

13. *clean*

14. *cry*

15. *listen to*

16. *yawn*

[ɪd]

17. *shout*

18. *paint*

19. *wait for*

20. *plant*

What's the Matter?

| I |
| We |
| You |
| They | } work every day. |

| He |
| She |
| It | } works every day. |

| I |
| We |
| You |
| They | } worked yesterday. |

| He |
| She |
| It |

A. How does David feel?

B. Not so good.

A. What's the matter?

B. He has a backache.

A. A backache? How did he get it?

B. He played basketball all day.*

*Or: He played basketball all morning/all afternoon/all evening/all night.

1. *Jane*

2. *George*

3. *you*

4. *Mary*

5. *Fred*

6. *you*

7. *Barbara*

8. *Mrs. Smith*

9. *you*

| eat – ate | sing – sang | drink – drank | sit – sat |

10. *Sally*

11. *Mario*

12. *you*

13. *Helen*

14. *you*

15. *Walter*

ON YOUR OWN: Do You Want to Make an Appointment?

You don't feel very well today. Call your doctor and make an appointment.

A. Hello, Doctor _____? This is

_____.

B. Hello, _____. How are you?

A. I don't feel very well today.

B. I'm sorry to hear that. What seems to be the problem?

A. I have a TERRIBLE _____.

B. Do you have any idea why?

A. Well, Doctor . . . I _____ all _____ yesterday.

B. I see. Do you want to make an appointment?

A. Yes, please. When can you see me?

B. How about tomorrow at _____ o'clock?

A. That's fine. Thank you very much.

THE WILSONS' PARTY

Mr. and Mrs. Wilson invited all their friends and neighbors to a party last night. They stayed home all day yesterday and prepared for the party.

In the morning the Wilsons worked outside. Their daughter, Margaret, cleaned the yard. Their son, Bob, painted the fence. Mrs. Wilson planted flowers in the garden, and Mr. Wilson fixed their broken front steps.

In the afternoon the Wilsons worked inside the house. Margaret washed the floors and vacuumed the living room carpet. Bob dusted the furniture and cleaned the basement. Mr. and Mrs. Wilson stayed in the kitchen all afternoon. He cooked spaghetti for dinner, and she baked apple pies for dessert.

The Wilsons finished all their work at six o'clock. Their house looked beautiful inside and out!

The Wilsons' guests arrived at about 7:30. After they arrived, they all sat in the living room. They ate cheese and crackers, drank wine, and talked. Some people talked about their children. Other people talked about the weather. And EVERYBODY talked about how beautiful the Wilsons' house looked inside and out!

The Wilsons served dinner in the dining room at 9:00. Everybody enjoyed the meal very much. They liked Mr. Wilson's spaghetti and they "loved" Mrs. Wilson's apple pie. In fact, everybody asked for seconds.

After dinner everybody sat in the living room again. First, Bob Wilson played the piano and his sister, Margaret, sang. Then, Mr. and Mrs. Wilson showed slides of their trip to Hawaii. After that, they turned on the stereo and everybody danced.

As you can see, the Wilsons' guests enjoyed the party very much. In fact, nobody wanted to go home!

✓ CHECK-UP

Answer These Questions

Answer using full sentences.

1. When did the guests arrive?
2. Where did the guests sit after they arrived?
3. What did they eat and drink before dinner?
4. What time did the Wilsons serve dinner?
5. What did Margaret do after dinner?

Listening

Listen and choose the word you hear.

1. a. study   b. studied
2. a. work   b. worked
3. a. stay   b. stayed
4. a. plant   b. planted
5. a. invite   b. invited
6. a. drink   b. drank
7. a. sit   b. sat
8. a. finish   b. finished
9. a. cook   b. cooked
10. a. eat   b. ate
11. a. watch   b. watched
12. a. clean   b. cleaned

✏ IN YOUR OWN WORDS

For Writing and Discussion

A PARTY

Tell about a party you enjoyed.

What did you eat?
What did you drink?
What did people do at the party?
   (eat, dance, talk about . . .)

CHAPTER 15 *SUMMARY*

GRAMMAR

Past Tense

I He She It We You They	worked yesterday.

[t]	I work**ed**. I danc**ed**.
[d]	I clean**ed** my apartment. I play**ed** cards.
[ɪd]	I rest**ed**. I shout**ed**.

Irregular Verbs

eat	–	ate
drink	–	drank
sing	–	sang
sit	–	sat

FUNCTIONS

Asking for and Reporting Information

How do you feel today?
How are you?
  I feel great/fine/okay.
  So-so.
  Not so good.
  I feel terrible.
  I don't feel very well today.

What's the matter?
What seems to be the problem?
  I have a *headache*.
  I have a terrible *headache*.

What did you do yesterday?
  I *worked*.

How *did he get a backache*?

Do you have any idea why?

Responding to Information

I'm glad to hear that.
I'm sorry to hear that.

Greeting People

Hello, Doctor _____? This is _____.
  Hello, _____.

Checking Understanding

A backache?

Indicating Understanding

I see.

Inquiring about Want-Desire

Do you want to *make an appointment*?

Inquiring about Ability

When can you *see me*?

Suggesting

How about *tomorrow at 2 o'clock*?
  That's fine.

Expressing Gratitude

Thank you very much.

Past Tense:
Yes/No Questions ▪
Short Answers ▪
WH-Questions ▪
More Irregular Verbs ▪
Time Expressions ▪

I Brushed My Teeth

I worked. I didn't work. (did not)	Did you work? Yes, I did. No, I didn't.

Today includes:

this morning
this afternoon
this evening
tonight

Yesterday includes:

yesterday morning
yesterday afternoon
yesterday evening
last night

1. Did he study English last night?

2. Did she wash her windows this morning?

3. Did you play the piano yesterday afternoon?

4. Did they call the doctor this afternoon?

5. Did she listen to records yesterday morning?

6. Did he clean his bedroom today?

We Went to the Supermarket

I went.
I didn't go.
(did not)

Did you go?
Yes, I did.
No, I didn't.

1. Did you go skating yesterday?
go – went

2. Did you take the subway this morning?
take – took

3. Did Steven get up at 10:00 this morning?
get – got

4. Did he have a stomachache last night?
have – had

5. Did Mrs. Smith buy bananas yesterday?
buy – bought

6. Did Tommy write to his grandmother this week?
write – wrote

7. Did you read a book this afternoon?
read – read

8. Did they do their homework last night?
do – did

Mary's Terrible Day

1. Mary went to a party last night.

2. She got up late today.

3. She missed the bus.

4. She had to walk to the office.

5. She arrived late for work.

6. Her boss shouted at her.

7. She had a bad headache all afternoon.

Complete this conversation, using the information above.

A. Hi, Mary! Did you have a good day today?

B. No, I didn't. I had a TERRIBLE day.

A. What happened?

B. I had a bad headache all afternoon.

A. Why did you have a bad headache?

B. Because my boss shouted at me.

A. Why did your boss shout at you?

B. Because I arrived late for work.

A. Why _____ late for work?

B. Because _____.

A. Why _____?

B. Because _____.

A. Why _____?

B. Because _____.

A. Why _____?

B. Because I went to a party last night.

How about YOU?

Did you go to a party last night?
What did you do last night?

Did you get up late today?
What time did you get up?

How did you get to class today?
Did you arrive on time?

Excuses

Are you sometimes late for class?
What do you usually tell your teacher?
Here are some excuses you can use the next time you're late.

I got up late.

I missed the _____. (bus/train/subway)

I had a _____ this morning. (stomachache/headache/. . .)

I had to go to the _____ before class. (post office/bank/doctor/
dentist/. . .)

I forgot* my _____ and had to go back home and get it. (English
book/pencil/. . .)

I met* _____ on the way to class. (an old friend/my cousin/. . .)

A thief stole* my _____. (car/bicycle/. . .)

Add some of your own excuses.

_____

_____

_____

*forget — forgot
  meet — met
  steal — stole

> **A.** I'm sorry I'm late.
>
> **B.** What happened? Did you get up late?
>
> **A.** No. I didn't get up late.
>
> **B.** Did you miss the bus?
>
> **A.** No. I didn't miss the bus.
>
> **B.** Well, why are you late?
>
> **A.** A thief stole my bicycle!
>
> **B.** Excuses! Excuses!

Now practice this conversation with other students in your class, using your own excuses.

> **A.** I'm sorry I'm late.
>
> **B.** What happened? Did _____?
>
> **A.** No. _____.
>
> **B.** Did _____?
>
> **A.** No. _____.
>
> **B.** Well, why are you late?
>
> **A.** _____.
>
> **B.** Excuses! Excuses!

LATE FOR WORK

Victor usually gets up at 7 A.M. He does his morning exercises for twenty minutes, takes a long shower, has a big breakfast, and leaves for work at 8 o'clock. He usually drives his car to work and gets there at 8:30.

This morning, however, he didn't get up at 7 A.M. He got up at 6 A.M. He didn't do his morning exercises for twenty mintues. He did them for only five minutes. He didn't take a long shower. He took a very quick shower. He didn't have a big breakfast. He had only a cup of coffee. He didn't leave for work at 8 o'clock. He left for work at 7.

Victor rushed out of the house an hour early this morning because his car is at the repair shop and he had to take the bus. He walked a mile from his house to the center of town. He waited fifteen minutes for the bus. And after he got off the bus, he walked half a mile to his factory.

Even though Victor got up early and rushed out of the house this morning, he didn't get to work on time. He got there forty-five minutes late and his supervisor got angry and shouted at him. Poor Victor! He really tried to get to work on time this morning.

CHECK-UP

Listening

Listen and write the missing words.

SHIRLEY'S DAY OFF

Shirley enjoyed her day off yesterday. She _____ late, _____ jogging in the park, _____ a long
1   2   3
shower, and _____ a big breakfast. In the afternoon,
4
she _____ to the movies with her sister, and in the
5
evening, she _____ dinner with her parents. After
6
dinner, they _____ in the living room and _____.
7   8
Shirley _____ a very pleasant day off yesterday.
9

Tell about a day off YOU enjoyed. What did you do in the morning? in the afternoon? in the evening?

GRAMMAR

Past Tense: Yes/No Questions

Did	I he she it we you they	work?

Short Answers

Yes,	I he she it we you they	did.

No,	I he she it we you they	didn't.

Past Tense: WH-Questions

What did	I he she it we you they	do?

Irregular Verbs

buy	bought
do	did
forget	forgot
get	got
go	went
have	had
meet	met
read	read
steal	stole
take	took
write	wrote

Time Expressions

Did you study English	yesterday? yesterday morning? yesterday afternoon? yesterday evening? last night?

FUNCTIONS

Asking for and Reporting Information

Did you *go to the bank this afternoon?*
  Yes, I did.
  No, I didn't.

Did you *have a good day today?*
  No, I didn't. *I had a TERRIBLE day.*

What happened?

Why did you *have a bad headache?*
  Because *my boss shouted at me.*

What did you do *last night?*
What time did you *get up?*
How did you *get to class today?*

I had a *stomachache this morning.*
I met *an old friend on the way to class.*

Expressing Obligation

I had to *go to the post office before class.*

Forgetting

I forgot *my English book.*

Apologizing

I'm sorry *I'm late.*

Greeting People

Hi, *Mary!*

To Be: Past Tense ▪

PRESTO Commercials

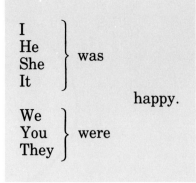

> I
> He
> She
> It
> } was
>
> happy.
>
> We
> You
> They
> } were

Before our family bought PRESTO Vitamins, we were always tired.

> I was tired.
> My wife was tired.
> My children were tired, too.

Now we're energetic, because WE bought PRESTO Vitamins. How about you?

Before our family bought _____, we were always _____.

> I was _____.
> My wife/husband was _____.
> My children were _____, too.

Now we're _____ because WE bought _____. How about you?

Using the above script, prepare commercials for these other fine PRESTO products.

1. *sad*   *happy*   2. *hungry*   *full*   3. *dirty*   *clean*

4. *sick*   *healthy*   5. *heavy*   *thin*   6. _____   _____

Before I Bought PRESTO Shampoo . . .

Before I bought PRESTO Shampoo, my hair **was** always dirty.   Now **it's** clean.

1. Before we bought PRESTO Toothpaste, our teeth _____ yellow. Now _____ white.

2. Before we bought PRESTO Paint, our house _____ ugly. Now _____ beautiful.

3. Before I bought PRESTO Furniture, I _____ uncomfortable. Now _____ very comfortable.

4. Before we bought PRESTO Dog Food, our dog _____ tiny. Now _____ enormous.

5. Before William bought PRESTO Window Cleaner, his windows _____ dirty. Now _____ clean.

6. Before Mr. and Mrs. Brown bought PRESTO Floor Wax, their kitchen floor _____ dull. Now _____ shiny.

Before I bought _____,

_____.

Now _____.

Were You at the Ballgame Last Night?

I He She It	wasn't (was not)
We You They	weren't (were not)

A. Were you at the ballgame last night?

B. No, I wasn't. I was at the movies.

1. Was it hot yesterday?

2. Were they at home this morning?

3. Was Betty sad yesterday?

4. Was your grandfather a dentist?

5. Were you at home last weekend?

6. Was I a quiet baby?

7. Was Richard on time for his plane?

8. Was Nancy late for the bus?

Did You Sleep Well Last Night?

I He She It We You They } did/didn't	I He She It } was/wasn't We You They } were/weren't

A. Did you sleep well last night?
B. Yes, I did. I was tired.

A. Did Roger sleep well last night?
B. No, he didn't. He wasn't tired.

1. **A.** Did Tom have a big breakfast today?
   B. Yes, _____. _____ hungry.

2. **A.** Did Jane have a big breakfast today?
   B. No, _____. _____ hungry.

3. **A.** Did Mrs. Brown go to the doctor yesterday?
   B. Yes, _____. _____ sick.

4. **A.** Did Mr. Brown go to the doctor yesterday?
   B. No, _____. _____ sick.

5. **A.** Did Timothy finish his milk?
   B. Yes, _____. _____ thirsty.

6. **A.** Did Jennifer finish her milk?
   B. No, _____. _____ thirsty.

7. **A.** Did Susan miss the train?
   B. Yes, _____. _____ late.

8. **A.** Did Sally miss the train?
   B. No, _____. _____ late.

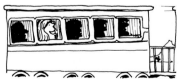

MARIA GOMEZ

Maria Gomez was born in Peru. She grew up in a small village. She began school when she was six years old. She went to elementary school, but she didn't go to high school. Her family was very poor, and she had to go to work when she was thirteen years old. She worked on an assembly line in a shoe factory.

When Maria was seventeen years old, her family moved to the United States. First they lived in Los Angeles, and then they moved to San Francisco. When Maria arrived in the United States, she wasn't very happy. She missed her friends back in Peru, and she didn't speak one word of English. She began to study English at night, and she worked in a factory during the day.

Maria studied very hard, and now she speaks English well. She's still studying at night, but now she's studying typing. She wants to be a secretary.

Maria still misses her friends back home. But she's very happy now, and she's looking forward to her future in her new country.

✓ CHECK-UP

Listening

Listen and choose the best answer based on the story.

1. a. In Peru.
   b. Maria Gomez.

2. a. When I was six years old.
   b. In a small village.

3. a. In a shoe factory.
   b. My family was very poor.

4. a. I wasn't very happy.
   b. We lived in Los Angeles.

5. a. Very hard.
   b. Typing.

IN YOUR OWN WORDS

For Writing and Discussion

Tell a story about yourself or someone in your family. In your story, answer questions such as:

Where were you born?
Where did you grow up?
Where did you go to school?
What did you study?
When did you move? Where?

$$\text{Yes,} \begin{cases} I \\ he \\ she \\ it \end{cases} \text{was.} \qquad \text{No,} \begin{cases} I \\ he \\ she \\ it \end{cases} \text{wasn't.} \qquad \text{Yes,} \begin{cases} I \\ he \\ she \\ it \\ we \\ you \\ they \end{cases} \text{did.} \qquad \text{No,} \begin{cases} I \\ he \\ she \\ it \\ we \\ you \\ they \end{cases} \text{didn't.}$$

$$\begin{cases} we \\ you \\ they \end{cases} \text{were.} \qquad \begin{cases} we \\ you \\ they \end{cases} \text{weren't.}$$

Answer these questions and then ask other students in your class.

1. What did you look like?
   Were you tall? thin? pretty? handsome? cute?
   Did you have curly hair? straight hair? long hair?
   Did you have dimples? freckles?

2. Did you have many friends?
   What did you do with your friends?
   What games did you play?

3. Did you like school?
   Who was your favorite teacher? Why?
   What was your favorite subject? Why?

4. What did you do in your spare time?
   Did you have a hobby?
   Did you play sports?

5. Who was your favorite hero?

6. How old were you when you began to talk?
   (I was _____ years old when I began to talk.)
   What were your first words?
   (My first words were _____.)

7. How old were you when you began to walk?

8. How old were you when you started school?

9. How old were you when you went on your first date?

Add three questions of your own and ask other students in your class.

10. _____?

11. _____?

12. _____?

GRAMMAR

To Be: Past Tense

I He She It	was	
We You They	were	happy.

I He She It	wasn't	
We You They	weren't	tired.

Was	I he she it	
Were	we you they	late?

Yes,	I he she it	was.
	we you they	were.

No,	I he she it	wasn't.
	we you they	weren't.

FUNCTIONS

Asking for and Reporting Information

How about you?

Were you *at the ballgame last night?*
  No, I wasn't. I was *at the movies.*

Did you *sleep well last night?*
  Yes, I did.
  No, I didn't.

Where were you born?
Where did you grow up?
Where did you go to school?
What did you study?
When did you move?
Where?
What did you look like?
What did you do *with your friends?*
How old were you when *you began to talk?*

Were you *tall?*
Did you have *curly hair?*

Inquiring about Likes/Dislikes

Did you like *school?*

Who was your favorite *teacher?*
What was your favorite *subject?*

Describing

We were always *sad.*
Now we're *happy.*

APPENDIX

Cardinal Numbers

1	one	20	twenty
2	two	21	twenty-one
3	three	22	twenty-two
4	four	.	.
5	five	.	.
6	six	29	twenty-nine
7	seven	30	thirty
8	eight	40	forty
9	nine	50	fifty
10	ten	60	sixty
11	eleven	70	seventy
12	twelve	80	eighty
13	thirteen	90	ninety
14	fourteen		
15	fifteen	100	one hundred
16	sixteen	200	two hundred
17	seventeen	300	three hundred
18	eighteen	.	.
19	nineteen	.	.
		900	nine hundred

1,000	one thousand
2,000	two thousand
3,000	three thousand
.	.
.	.
10,000	ten thousand
100,000	one hundred thousand
1,000,000	one million

Ordinal Numbers

1st	first	20th	twentieth
2nd	second	21st	twenty-first
3rd	third	22nd	twenty-second
4th	fourth	.	.
5th	fifth	.	.
6th	sixth	29th	twenty-ninth
7th	seventh	30th	thirtieth
8th	eighth	40th	fortieth
9th	ninth	50th	fiftieth
10th	tenth	60th	sixtieth
11th	eleventh	70th	seventieth
12th	twelfth	80th	eightieth
13th	thirteenth	90th	ninetieth
14th	fourteenth		
15th	fifteenth	100th	one hundredth
16th	sixteenth	1,000th	one thousandth
17th	seventeenth	1,000,000th	one millionth
18th	eighteenth		
19th	nineteenth		

How to read a date:
June 9, 1941 = "June ninth, nineteen forty-one"

Irregular Verbs: Past Tense

be	was	have	had
buy	bought	meet	met
do	did	read	read
drink	drank	sing	sang
eat	ate	sit	sat
forget	forgot	steal	stole
get	got	take	took
go	went	write	wrote

Tape Scripts for Listening Exercises

Chapter 1 – p. 5
Listen and choose the best answer.
1. A. What's your name?
   B. Susan Miller.
2. A. What's your address?
   B. Three ninety-four Main Street.
3. A. What's your apartment number?
   B. Nine D.
4. A. What's your telephone number?
   B. Seven four eight – two two six oh.
5. A. What's your Social Security number?
   B. Oh six oh – eight three – eight two seven five.

Chapter 2 – p. 13
Listen and choose the best answer.
1. Mr. Jones is in the park.
2. Betty is in the library.
3. He's in the kitchen.
4. She's in the living room.
5. They're in the yard.
6. We're in the basement.

Chapter 3 – p. 21
Listen and choose the best answer.
1. What are you doing?
2. What's Mr. Smith doing?
3. What's Mrs. Larson doing?
4. What are Bill and Mary doing?
5. What are you and Henry doing?
6. What am I drinking?

Chapter 4 – p. 29
Listen and choose the best answer.
1. What are you painting?
2. What are you playing?
3. What are they reading?
4. What is she eating?
5. What is he washing?
6. What are you watching?

Chapter 5 – p. 39
Listen and choose the best answer.
1. How's the weather?
2. Tell me about your hotel.
3. How are the children?
4. Tell me about your boyfriend.
5. Tell me about your new apartment.
6. How's your new car?

Chapter 6 – p. 47
Listen to the sentence. Are the people quiet or noisy?
1. They're listening to loud music.
2. I'm reading.
3. She's sleeping.
4. The band is playing.
5. Everybody is singing and dancing.
6. He's studying.

Chapter 7 – p. 59
What words do you hear?
Ex.: My neighborhood is very nice. There's a park nearby, and there's a drug store around the corner.
1. My neighborhood is very convenient. There's a bank around the corner and a restaurant across the street.
2. My neighborhood is very noisy. There's a gas station next to my building, and there's a police station across the street.
3. The sidewalks in my neighborhood are very busy. There's a school across the street and a department store around the corner.
4. There's a big shopping mall outside my city. There's a toy store and a movie theater in the mall.
5. There are many small stores in the center of my town. There's a bakery, a shoe store, and a clothing store.

Chapter 8 – p. 69
Listen and choose the word you hear.
1. These ties are plain.
2. This jacket is dirty.
3. Excuse me. I'm looking for a cotton blouse.
4. I'm wearing my new socks.
5. Is this your boot?
6. Purple umbrellas are very popular.

Chapter 9 – p. 76
Listen and choose the best answer.
1. What does she read?
2. What does she eat?
3. What do they watch?
4. What do they wash?
5. What do you sing?
6. What do you drink?

Chapter 10 – p. 85
Choose the best answer to finish the sentence.
1. A. Do I speak English very well?
   B. Yes, . . .
2. A. Does Mr. Miller live in Toronto?
   B. No, . . .
3. A. Does your brother work in New York?
   B. Yes, . . .
4. A. Do you and your wife clean the house together?
   B. Yes, . . .
5. A. Do your neighbors work in their garden?
   B. No, . . .
6. A. Does your grandmother talk about life back in "the old country"?
   B. Yes, . . .
7. A. Do you go to school on the weekend?
   B. No, . . .
8. A. Does she live in this neighborhood?
   B. No, . . .

Chapter 11 – p. 95
Who and what are they talking about?
1. A. How often do you see her?
   B. I see her every day.
2. A. How often do you wash them?
   B. I wash them every year.
3. A. Do you write to him very often?
   B. Yes. I write to him every week.
4. A. Is it broken?
   B. Yes. He's fixing it now.
5. A. I see them all the time.
   B. That's nice.
6. A. I rarely visit him.
   B. Oh, really?

Chapter 12 – p. 102
Listen and choose the best answer.
1. What are you doing?
2. What does the secretary do?
3. What is the receptionist doing?
4. Is he angry?
5. What do you do when you're sick?

Chapter 13 – p. 109
I. Listen and circle.
1. I can speak English.
2. He can't swim.
3. They can't ski.
4. She can play the piano.
5. We can dance.
6. I can't type.

II. Choose what each person can do.
1. I can sing. I can't dance.
2. He can't file. He can type.
3. She can't fix motors. She can repair locks.
4. He can cook. He can't bake.
5. I can drive a truck. I can't drive a bus.
6. She can't teach history. She can teach science.

Chapter 14 – p. 120
Listen and choose the words you hear.
1. A. When are you going to visit me?
   B. Next month.
2. A. When are you going to begin your vacation?
   B. This Sunday.
3. A. When is your son going to call my daughter?
   B. This afternoon.
4. A. When are your neighbors going to move?
   B. Next November.
5. A. When is she going to get her driver's license?
   B. Next week.
6. A. When are you going to do your laundry?
   B. This evening.
7. A. When are we going to go to the concert?
   B. This Thursday.
8. A. When is your daughter going to finish college?
   B. Next winter.
9. A. When are you going to buy a car?
   B. Tomorrow.
10. A. When is the landlord going to fix the window?
    B. At once.

Chapter 15 – p. 133
Listen and choose the word you hear.
1. I studied at the library all day.
2. We work at the restaurant all day.
3. They stayed home all afternoon.
4. I plant flowers in my garden in the spring.
5. They invited their friends to their parties.
6. Mr. and Mrs. Franklin drink lemonade all summer.
7. Tim and Bill sat in their living room all morning.
8. They finish their work at four o'clock.
9. Mr. Wilson cooked dinner for his family.
10. The people at the party ate cheese and crackers.
11. She watched TV in the living room.
12. He cleaned the basement every day.

Chapter 16 – p. 141
Listen and write the missing words.
Shirley enjoyed her day off yesterday. She got up late, went jogging in the park, took a long shower, and ate a big breakfast. In the afternoon, she went to the movies with her sister, and in the evening, she had dinner with her parents. After dinner they sat in the living room and talked. Shirley had a very pleasant day off yesterday.

Chapter 17 – p. 148
Listen and choose the best answer based on the story.
1. Maria, where were you born?
2. When did you begin school?
3. Why did you go to work when you were thirteen?
4. How did you feel when you arrived in the United States?
5. What are you studying now?

Glossary

The number after each word indicates the page where the word first appears.
(adj) = adjective, (adv) = adverb, (n) = noun, (v) = verb.